He was glaring at the snow from his cashmere coat, his icy blue eyes the only element of light in his shadowed face.

"You could have joined our driver and stayed at one of the local crofts, if this place doesn't meet with your satisfaction."

"Don't try and be clever, Flora. I have things I'm supposed to be doing and places I'm supposed to be, namely on a skiing trip in Switzerland with friends, not stuck on some god-forsaken estate in the middle of nowhere with..."

"It's Christmas, Vito," Flora said, hugging her arms around herself to try to generate some heat. "Most people have places to be. Even me," she added.

But despite her reasonable tone, her heart was racing as she tried to get her head around her current reality.

She was trapped with Vito Monticello.

Stuck in a snowstorm, in the middle of nowhere with her fierce and sexy boss.

Sharon Kendrick once won a national writing competition by describing her ideal date: being flown to an exotic island by a gorgeous and powerful man. Little did she realize that she'd just wandered into her dream job! Today, she writes for Harlequin, and her books feature often stubborn but always to-die-for heroes and the women who bring them to their knees. She believes that the best books are those you never want to end. Just like life...

Books by Sharon Kendrick

Harlequin Presents

Secrets of Cinderella's Awakening
Confessions of His Christmas Housekeeper
Her Christmas Baby Confession
Innocent Maid for the Greek
Italian Nights to Claim the Virgin
The Housekeeper's One-Night Baby
The King's Hidden Heir
His Enemy's Italian Surrender
Greek's Bartered Bride

Jet-Set Billionaires

Penniless and Pregnant in Paradise

Passionately Ever After...

Stolen Nights with the King

Visit the Author Profile page
at Harlequin.com for more titles.

CHRISTMAS WITH CONSEQUENCES

SHARON KENDRICK

PRESENTS

If you purchased this book without a cover you should be aware that this book is stolen property. It was reported as "unsold and destroyed" to the publisher, and neither the author nor the publisher has received any payment for this "stripped book."

ISBN-13: 978-1-335-21325-9

Recycling programs for this product may not exist in your area.

Christmas with Consequences

Copyright © 2025 by Sharon Kendrick

All rights reserved. No part of this book may be used or reproduced in any manner whatsoever without written permission.

Without limiting the author's and publisher's exclusive rights, any unauthorized use of this publication to train generative artificial intelligence (AI) technologies is expressly prohibited.

This is a work of fiction. Names, characters, places and incidents are either the product of the author's imagination or are used fictitiously. Any resemblance to actual persons, living or dead, businesses, companies, events or locales is entirely coincidental.

For questions and comments about the quality of this book, please contact us at CustomerService@Harlequin.com.

TM and ® are trademarks of Harlequin Enterprises ULC.

Harlequin Enterprises ULC
22 Adelaide St. West, 41st Floor
Toronto, Ontario M5H 4E3, Canada
www.Harlequin.com

Printed in Lithuania

CHRISTMAS WITH CONSEQUENCES

To all my readers—that great global community of romance-lovers, who enjoy reading my books as much as I enjoy writing them.

This one's for you. xxx

CHAPTER ONE

Her head thudding with worry about the days ahead—even though Christmas was supposed to be a *happy* time—Flora was more preoccupied than usual as she pushed open the door.

She looked around, frantically trying to work out what was different, apart from the newly purchased strands of tinsel and the artificial tree she'd brought from the market because Julian had demanded it (although this year mistletoe had been banned in the workplace). She gave a little nod. So far, so seasonal.

It was only as she ventured further into the cavernous interior of the huge room that she noticed what was missing.

Like, just about *everything*.

Gone were the silver-framed photos of the neglected wife of her boss, and the children he never really saw. Gone was that expensive painting of London which had dominated the wall behind the desk and which she'd never really liked. The heavy paperweight which had looked like an instrument of assassination had also disappeared and so too had the hat which had always hung—pristine and unworn—on the coat stand. The place looked bare—almost as if it had been *ransacked*—and the untidy spill of expensive pens lying scattered over the floor only added to that impression, as if their owner had left in a hurry.

But before she'd even had a chance to bend and pick them up, Flora heard a sound behind her and turned around, her heart clenching beneath her thin blouse when she saw the man who was framed in the doorway.

Reality took another strange shift, because instead of the corpulent frame of her boss, before her stood a vision of...

Of what?

She blinked. She, who was normally so exacting, had found what she had never expected to find.

Perfection.

Six foot two and eyes of blue.

Flora's throat grew dry and suddenly she was having difficulty swallowing because she'd never seen anyone like him.

The man's physical beauty was so bright that you almost wanted to cram on a pair of sunglasses to protect your eyes from the incandescence he radiated. But someone had once told her that you should never trust first impressions and Flora had believed them. Because beneath his flawless exterior there was something which hinted at hidden depths and danger—and she was someone who ran a million miles from danger. He reminded her of one of those prowling jaguars you sometimes saw on wildlife programmes—strong beasts which dominated their surroundings, no matter how hard they tried to blend into the background.

And this was not a man who *blended*.

The sophisticated cut of his suit did nothing to disguise the hard body beneath and his shadowed jaw was firm and uncompromising. His skin gleamed like burnished gold—contrasting with coal-black hair and matching lashes, which framed eyes of the most incredible shade of blue. Eyes like chips of aquamarine were studying her with a cool and not particularly friendly appraisal.

Flora gave a jolt as she found herself reacting to him on a weird and purely physical level. She could feel it prickling hotly over her skin, like the start of a fever. Pushing through her veins like honey. A tug of something sweet and warm and forbidden low in her belly.

Suddenly, she became painfully aware of the fact that her hair was unflatteringly damp from the shower and her cheeks were burning from the physical exertion of getting here. She knew she was staring at him like an idiot and yet somehow she couldn't seem to tear her eyes away, even as she watched the sensual curve of his lips hardening into a cynical slash.

As if he were used to women finding him fascinating.

As if the predictability of such behaviour bored him.

'Didn't your mother teach you it was rude to stare?' he taunted softly.

His mocking words punctured her unwanted fantasy and Flora was grateful to be able to focus on something other than the bizarre effect he was having on her. Her mother had taught her plenty of things—just not the kinds of things that mothers were *supposed* to teach. She'd known all about excitement and living on the edge.

And danger, of course. She had excelled at that. She just hadn't been very good at showing her daughters the most sensible way to navigate your way through life.

Everything Flora knew, she had learnt herself, the hard way—and the most important lesson of all was that actions had consequences. So although instinct made her want to answer this distractingly gorgeous man with a flippant retort, experience made her bite it back. Was that because there was something awfully *imperious* about his manner which was making her feel apprehensive, though she couldn't work out why?

'Why wouldn't I stare?' she questioned reasonably. 'You scared me. Creeping up on me like that.'

'*Creeping?*' he echoed furiously. 'You are inferring that I am some kind of stalker?'

'Perhaps that was the wrong word,' she amended quickly. 'I just wasn't expecting anyone to be here.'

'But it is almost nine o'clock,' he observed, glancing at the gold watch which gleamed beneath one pristine cuff, his richly accented voice sounding like iron shavings shot with silk. 'What time does your boss usually start work?'

That would depend on what he'd been doing the night before, Flora thought, though she didn't say so. For someone who looked like a walking health hazard and never bothered to remove the golden wedding band which dug into his fleshy finger, Julian Wootton was surprisingly successful with the opposite sex—probably because he was prone to spending obscene amounts of money on them. How many times had Flora been instructed to send flowers or air tickets as farewell gifts to his discarded lovers, or—if the woman was being particularly tricky and demanding he get a divorce—costly jewels?

She glanced down at the pens still strewn on the silk rug as the bizarreness of the situation began to reassert itself and when she looked up again she realised that the man's cold gaze was still fixed on her. And really, why was she letting some complete stranger come in here and start throwing his weight around?

'Excuse me, but who *are* you?' she said, knowing this was something she should have verified the moment he set foot in the office, rather than standing there drooling like a starving dog confronted by a juicy bone. Clearing her throat, she attempted to inject her voice with authority, which she tempered with a polite smile. 'This is the office of Julian Wootton, the CEO and he has no meetings in his diary for this morning. Unless he's scheduled something and forgotten to tell me.'

As she studied him questioningly, Vito felt another flicker of the irritation which had been hovering perilously close to the surface ever since his private jet had touched down, just as dawn had finished streaking the London sky. His ego certainly didn't need massaging and he wasn't someone who ever sought recognition, though in his native Italy that had always been a big ask—given his high-profile and infuriating reputation as one of the country's most eligible bachelors. For this reason he usually embraced anonymity with enthusiasm, but...

He frowned.

Didn't the fact that this woman didn't know him reinforce how much he had taken his eye off the ball lately, and all the reasons why? He felt the twist of pain and self-recrimination, followed inevitably by the tang of regret. Always regret, he thought bitterly. As stubborn and unshiftable as the blame which accompanied it, whenever he thought about his brother.

Ruffled by this unwanted ambush of emotion, Vito sought to distract himself. Should he play a little game with her? he wondered cruelly. Pretend to be some hapless Italian who had wandered out of the elevator at the wrong floor and allow her to patronise him by speaking *very slowly*. Or make her day by flirting a little? Judging by the way she'd been staring at him, it wouldn't take very long to have her eating out of his hand.

But, even if this wasn't business—and he never combined business with pleasure—she wasn't the kind of woman he'd ever flirt with. He took in her damp and slightly frizzy russet hair. The rosy apples of her rounded cheeks. The cheap white blouse and utilitarian skirt which hinted at abundant curves beneath. He gave a disbelieving little shake of his head.

'My name is Vito Monticello,' he said quietly and saw from the way her lips framed her sudden shock that now she knew exactly who he was.

'Oh, my...' The shock became a wobbly smile as she held back what was obviously an exclamation of horror. 'You're the boss?'

'The owner,' he corrected bluntly. 'Of the company which employs you, Miss...?'

'Greening,' she answered, clearly very flustered now.

'Flora Greening. I'm so sorry I didn't recognise you, but I thought…'

'What?' he queried and when she shrugged her shoulders, repeated silkily. 'What did you think, Miss Greening?'

'That you'd be…'

He raised his eyebrows in mocking query.

'Older,' she admitted. 'And I wasn't…expecting you. I mean, there was no warning you were coming here.'

He gave a wolfish smile. 'That's because I didn't give any.'

Her head was darting from side to side as if she were expecting her boss to suddenly leap out from behind a piece of furniture.

'Where's Julian?' she asked.

'I've fired him.'

Her expression grew even more mortified and all at once he forgot the frizzy hair and the flushed cheeks, the ugly skirt and cheap blouse. Because her widened eyes were the most extraordinary colour, he realised, with a sudden unexpected punch to the heart. They were green and shot with gold, like sunlight falling onto the first leaves of spring.

'Oh my goodness!' She cleared her throat again, her next question coming out as a husky whisper. 'Why did you do that?'

Impatient with the crazy trajectory of his thoughts—because since when did his heart ever miss a beat over some frumpy secretary's *eyes*?—Vito glared at her. 'Are you telling me you're surprised that I've let go of such a towering captain of industry?' he drawled sarcastically.

'Ah, I can see you're reluctant to answer that particular question. Perhaps you're worried about incriminating yourself?'

'Of course I'm not!'

'Then I suggest you stop biting your lip like a nervous exam student and sit down so I can ask you a few questions,' he instructed, his finger pointing towards the chair in front of the desk. 'Over there, if you like.'

She surveyed the proffered chair warily. 'Honestly, I'm quite happy to stand. Or...' She looked at him hopefully. 'Perhaps I could get you a cup of coffee, Mr Monticello?'

'It's *Signor* Monticello,' he corrected waspishly. 'And no, you can't.' Did she think he could be placated with a warm drink of some unspeakable brew he had been served so many times outside his native Italy? 'I drank some on the plane which is always mixed to my particular specification. And what's more, I don't appreciate what is obviously a stalling tactic in order to avoid what will probably be a difficult conversation. Do you understand what I'm saying, Miss Greening?'

'I understand perfectly. You have made your position abundantly clear, Signor Monticello.' She was blinking at him now—those long lashes fluttering over the amazing eyes like a pair of distracted butterflies. But she slid obediently into the seat he had suggested, her hands clasped together on her lap as she fixed her gaze on him.

'Okay, let's begin,' he said, wondering why her hair was so damp when it wasn't raining. 'How long have you worked for Julian Wootton?'

Flora clasped and unclasped her hands, suspecting

he already knew the answer to this particular question, but also knowing that she wanted to humour him. She *had* to. He wasn't just drop-dead gorgeous, he was rich and powerful. He was also her boss and he held her future in his hands. Oh, *why* hadn't she recognised him? But she knew exactly why. He'd taken over after the death of his father a year ago, just after she'd joined the company, when everything had seemed so new and scarily different after her many contented years in the library. But that was all she did know about him. She made it her business to learn the names of everyone who worked in the building—from the cleaners to the executive board—because she liked as many facts as possible at her fingertips and then she liked to file them neatly in her mind.

But during her lunch-break she nearly always had her nose in a book and kept herself to herself. She certainly didn't gossip with the other people who worked at the London headquarters of Verdenergia, who might have informed her that Vito Monticello looked like a god. She knew very well that the other women at the multinational energy company—and the men too, most probably—regarded her as something of a freak, but Flora didn't care. Her experience had been so different to that of other people her age. Her teenage years had gifted her the legacy of feeling like a permanent outsider. Which she was. But that was okay and she was cool with it.

Shifting uncomfortably in her seat, she prayed Vito Monticello would be gentle with her. That he wasn't on a mission to catch her out. Would he see her as the tainted ally of the man he'd just fired and dispatch her with similar speed and ruthlessness?

Because it would be easy to catch her out, wouldn't it? She certainly wasn't labouring under any illusion that she was nothing but a glorified diary keeper, who kept all the balls spinning in the air when her boss was too hung-over to deal with them himself. And yes, recently her conscience had been protesting that she needed to get herself a different job with better prospects which would make her feel more excited about going into work in the morning, and she was planning to do exactly that.

But not now.

Not yet.

Not with Christmas just around the corner.

The money was too good, and there was Amy...

Sucking in a deep breath, Flora willed herself to relax because she wasn't going to think about Amy. Not with that granite-faced man scowling at her. She wasn't going to risk exposing any of her stupid vulnerabilities to him. She wasn't going to risk *anything*. She never had and never would. She swallowed. She'd learnt from bitter experience that risk was a fool's game.

'I've worked here for just over a year.'

'And before that?'

Resisting the desire to suggest it might be simpler if he simply read her CV, Flora met his piercing blue gaze. 'I was a classroom assistant, and then I worked in a library.'

'*Si?*' he said softly, his ebony gaze sweeping over her. 'That figures. You look like a librarian.'

Flora tried not to react to his drawled comment because she knew exactly what it meant. The term was code. A subtext. It implied she conformed perfectly to the stereotype of a buttoned-up woman. The sort who would never say boo to a goose, or worry if her skirt was the wrong length to ever be fashionable. But she didn't really care because she *was* that woman, and so what? Life was safer if you had a protective shield to hide behind. And what right did he have to judge her past? 'It was a very fulfilling job,' she added defensively.

'I'm sure it was.' He ran a slow thumb over the curve of his jaw, drawing her attention to the faint shadow which made him look so darkly virile. As if she needed any reminding!

'I'm just surprised, that's all,' he continued. 'Stamping books and imposing fines doesn't seem a natural pathway to becoming a personal assistant to the chief executive officer of a large, energy company.' He paused. 'What made you leave the library if you liked it so much?'

She shrugged. 'It was shut down.'

'Why?'

As Flora met his uncomprehending stare, a sense of exasperation rose within her. What would he know of the plight of ordinary folk—this suited and booted billionaire, who had probably been born with a silver spoon in his mouth? Shouldn't she enlighten him about the ways of the world before he silkily informed her that her services were no longer required? 'Cuts,' she informed him briskly, her voice growing a little unsteady. 'The government had to reduce their spending—and said they could no longer justify funding the local library because more and more people were using screens.'

'But you didn't agree with them?'

'Of course I didn't agree with them!' she declared and all the pent-up emotions she'd been trying so hard to suppress for weeks now came bubbling to the surface. 'Yes, screens are in the majority these days but nothing ever beats the magic of a book. Yet some children are brought up in households where they never even see one,' she added, unable to keep the outrage from her voice. 'And libraries are a lifeline to people who can't afford to buy them!'

Vito's eyes narrowed, unexpectedly impressed—and surprised—by her impassioned outburst. It seemed the mousy secretary had fire. And substance. He knew about her background of course—he'd flicked through her CV on the plane over, when he'd been examining the activities of her boss. Apparently she was extremely diligent and hard-working, and her worthy defence of the underprivileged seemed genuine, and commendable. She looked—and sounded—like the kind of person he would instinctively trust.

But Vito had spent much of his life surrounded by people who were not what they seemed. Who pretended to be something other than what they really were. And that, along with the ridiculous amount of wealth he had acquired and which had turned him into a target for so many wannabes, made him naturally suspicious. Especially of women, whom he had always found to be particularly disingenuous. He chose his words carefully, his gaze steady as he delivered them. 'Were you aware that Julian Wootton was totally incompetent?'

She sat up very straight. 'It's not my role to judge my boss.'

'Perhaps you colluded with him?' he continued, his silky tone inviting confidence and—possibly—indiscretion. 'I've heard that he was unexpectedly popular with the ladies.'

Her apple-round cheeks were bright with indignation. 'I find that a very offensive accusation, *Signor* Monticello.'

He let her heated words bounce off him, with a shrug. 'It would be remiss of me not to enquire.'

'I suppose so,' she agreed reluctantly.

'So as far as you were concerned, he was an efficient boss, under whose guidance this giant industrial ship sailed without mishap through the choppiest of waters. Ah! I see that you are biting your lip again, Miss Greening—something which I observe you do when feeling a little uncomfortable.'

'How on earth could you possibly know something like that?' she questioned, her cheeks becoming even more flushed. 'When we've only been acquainted for a manner of minutes!'

'Because I am good at reading people,' he murmured. Especially women. Although possibly not a woman like this, he conceded to himself, as she brushed a damp strand of hair away from a flushed cheek totally devoid of make-up.

Marshalling the unusual direction of his thoughts, he went to stand by the window, staring down at the street below which was just beginning to get busy. Workers were streaming from the nearby Tube station towards the offices and shops which awaited them, and lights were twinkling in the windows. Far more lights than usual, he concluded grimly—for the kaleidoscopic display cutting through the grey of the December morning could mean only one thing.

Christmas.

Vito's jaw tightened.

It was a festival he had never enjoyed, because of the slew of messy memories which accompanied it. The inevitable fight between his parents about whose 'turn' it was to have the boys. The parties and alcohol which made his mother's behaviour especially unpredictable after the divorce—so that it wouldn't be *Babbo Natale* who Vito expected to see on Christmas Eve, but strange men creeping down the staircase of their villa in Rome, carrying their shoes.

At least as an adult he had found a surefire escape route during the holidays, saying a silent prayer of thanks for skiing. For the thrills and danger, the black runs and hard, physical exercise which left him no time to think. Once he had concluded his business here, he would be free for the holidays, which he would spend as far away from civilisation as possible. The garish bright lights of Christmas would be replaced by the pristine beauty of Gstaad and afterwards he would return to Italy, to a quieter world.

Turning back, he saw the secretary watching him closely, those astonishing eyes half shaded by her long lashes, her hands still clasped in her lap.

'So you had absolutely no idea that Wootton was failing to do his job properly?' he demanded.

'I...'

He saw the look of indecision which flitted across her face and felt the flicker of challenge. 'Let's get one thing straight, shall we, Miss Greening?' he suggested softly. 'You should forget about displaying any misplaced loyalty towards Wootton. I see little point in this interview progressing, unless you intend being scrupulously honest with me.' He paused. 'Were you or were you not aware that he was failing to do his job properly?'

Flora felt as if she were on a dissecting table, being filleted by Vito Monticello's laser-like gaze and the cutting edge of his words. She wanted to tell him that her boss's transgressions were nothing to do with her and surely she shouldn't be expected to deliver a verdict on his capabilities.

But if she didn't cooperate, then Vito Monticello *might* sack her and that was the last thing she could cope with, and not just because Christmas was an expensive time of year. Imagine having no job to go to. A world with no structure, or demands on her time. Just empty days, alone with her thoughts—and the long, winter nights ahead.

'Obviously, I was aware that Mr Wootton sometimes arrived late and occasionally took longer for lunch than some of the other directors,' she offered stiffly.

'And you covered for him?' he demanded.

'Of course I covered for him!' she protested. 'That's part of being a secretary—making your boss's life run smoothly.'

'Even when he's abusing his position?' His blue gaze

was cold. 'You didn't think of mentioning it to someone else? One of the other directors, perhaps?'

Suddenly Flora had had enough of this hostile interrogation. The Italian billionaire was obviously working up to getting rid of her, so why not speak the total truth, which he *claimed* he wanted to hear?

Drawing her shoulders back, she met his accusing gaze. 'And how would that have worked?' she demanded. 'Should I have requested a meeting with the CFO to tell them that, with my vast experience of one whole year in the business, I thought the chief executive wasn't up to scratch? Don't you have any understanding of the concept of hierarchy, Signor Monticello, and how it works?'

Unexpectedly, he laughed—as if her response wasn't what he had been expecting. But then his handsome face darkened again.

'*Colpa mia*, but I haven't been paying proper attention,' he said, half to himself and for a full half minute he seemed to be totally preoccupied with his thoughts, before narrowing his intense gaze at her so that his eyes resembled slivers of blue glass. 'Look, do you want this job, or not?'

Flora took a moment before answering. 'I need this job,' she said carefully. 'At least until after the New Year, when I might be able to find something which suits me better.'

He didn't react or ask why, and she was grateful for his indifference because how pathetic would it have sounded if she'd blurted out the truth?

My baby sister is getting married and going to the other end of the world and I'm going to miss her like hell.

It sounded pathetic, even to her.

'Okay. So let me tell you what's going to happen,' he said softly. 'If you work for me you need to know I have certain rules. You work all the hours I tell you to work, and you will be compensated accordingly. If you've got a date and I need you, you cancel it, understand?'

No need to tell him she didn't have a cat's chance in hell of having a date. Instead, Flora nodded. 'Yes.'

'You never talk to the press and you never put them through to me. If they have a query about the company, direct them straight to the PR team. Understand?'

'Yes,' she said again.

'Someone from one of my other companies is arriving later to take over the day-to-day running of the company, while I find a permanent replacement for your boss. In the meantime, I intend to let everyone know that things are going to be very different from now on.' His eyes narrowed. 'I assume you know everyone who works here?'

'I do.'

'Good.' He nodded his jet-black head. 'I want you to fill me in about every single employee in the building, and then I want to meet them. Afterwards you're going to take me through the diary, page by page. Is there anything particularly pressing I should know about?'

Flora nodded, feeling on slightly safer ground now that he'd stopped firing out a series of demands. 'There's the new advertising campaign for household insulation coming up, and of course, the opening of our new wind farm,' she added, unable to keep the note of pride from her voice because she had organised the entire thing.

'When's that?'

'On the twenty-third of December, sir. I know it's very close to Christmas—'

He silenced her with a wave of his hand. '*Si*. I can fit that in before I fly out to Switzerland,' he observed, almost thoughtfully.

Flora sat up straight, because maybe he would value initiative as well as honesty. 'Or you could always send the CFO in your place?' she suggested.

'That isn't going to happen because I've sacked him too.' He gave another wolfish smile. 'So I'll be going to Scotland and you will be coming with me.'

'Me, sir?'

'*Si*. And don't call me sir,' he instructed testily. 'My name is Vito. Got that?' He gave a dismissive nod of his head. 'You can go now.'

He plucked a vibrating cell phone from his suit jacket and flicked it a quick glance, replacing it without answering it, and she had just reached the door when his next silken words halted her. 'Oh, and, Flora?'

She turned around, wondering what else he was going to ask of her. 'Yes...Vito?'

His handsome face had darkened with irritation and he was jabbing an accusing finger towards the sapphire tinsel which was draped extravagantly around the front of the desk. 'Get rid of these damned decorations, will you?'

CHAPTER TWO

'I don't want to go,' Flora said stubbornly.

'Why not?' Perched on the bar-stool in the cramped kitchen of their Ealing flat, Amy swung her thick blond plait over her shoulder and looked at her sister incredulously. 'A trip to Scotland with your hot, billionaire boss on his private jet. What's not to like?'

Flora was about to blurt out that the thought of being incarcerated with an arrogant man like Vito Monticello for any amount of time was horrific, but she quickly clamped her lips shut. Amy might worry and it had always been her default setting to keep her little sister free from care.

And anyway, it wasn't strictly true, was it? Mostly her aversion was more to do with her own feelings and her inexplicable reaction to someone who was so far out of her orbit that he might as well have hailed from a completely different universe. What had happened today had felt crazy. And weird. He made her aware of her body in a way that had never happened before.

'I don't particularly want to get on a private jet with him,' she told her sister calmly. 'For a start, it's right before the holidays.'

'And?' Amy drummed her fingernails on the kitchen counter impatiently. 'You'll be back in time for Christmas Day, won't you?'

Well, yes, of course she would be—but that wasn't the point. Flora felt flustered as she tried to hold back a sudden rush of emotion, not wanting to swamp the baby chick she'd cared for ever since their mother had fallen to her death while rock climbing, a sport she had pursued to the exclusion of everything else—even her own children. Amy had been only ten and Flora a mere eight years older when they'd been brutally orphaned, and it had been a tough battle to convince social services she was capable of being a stand-in mum. But she'd done it. Somehow. She'd managed to create a warm and cosy little nest on a shoestring budget. She'd fitted her life around the grieving little girl and had nurtured her, fiercely contradicting anyone who ever praised her for making 'sacrifices'. Because that word hadn't even figured on her radar.

She'd done it out of love.

Yet sometimes the fear which had underpinned that love had terrified her.

It still did.

She was so proud of her younger sister. The way she'd entered nursing at eighteen and shown a real aptitude for the caring profession. Meeting an Aussie doctor and getting engaged just before she qualified hadn't been part of anyone's vision, and though Flora was delighted that Amy had found love, that didn't stop her fretting. She was so *young*—just twenty-one. And she was going such a long way away. But thoughts like that were selfish and she mustn't allow them head space.

'I was hoping to be here in the run-up to the holidays to do all the prep,' she husked. 'It's going to be your last one here, after all.'

'Rubbish!' negated her sister. 'I'm only going to be a plane ride away. And you'll be coming out to Brisbane for turkey on the beach next year, remember? Anyway, Brett and I can do Christmas for *you* for a change! We'd love to.' She beamed. 'And when you get back from Scotland you won't have to lift a finger.'

Flora did her best to appear happy, especially as Amy seemed to be so excited about the prospect. Perhaps she and Brett would welcome a bit of personal space in the cramped Ealing apartment for once. Did they sometimes think that three was a crowd—and that she was a bit of a gooseberry who cramped their style?

And wasn't she?

It seemed to go even further downhill from there. Usually, Flora loved the run-up to Christmas—but this year it seemed to pass her by and there was only one person responsible. Vito Monticello's killjoy attitude had extended far beyond his own vast office and, during his first few days of prowling around his London empire, had demanded the removal of every single Christmas decoration in the Verdenergia building. The tall conifer tree which decorated the shiny marble foyer had been the only thing which had been allowed to remain and even that had been after a battle, when Flora had explained that sometimes she saw little children stopping to look at it, their noses pressed against the window.

'Oh, very well,' he had conceded, with an impatient sigh. 'But everything else goes, understand?'

'If you insist. But people won't be very happy about it.'

His jet brows had been elevated in arrogant query as he awaited an explanation.

'For the past few months all the staff have been making their offices into little grottos,' Flora informed him weakly. 'It's a company tradition, apparently.'

'*Peccato*,' he snapped. 'Too bad. Let them create their *little grottos* at home. It's a fire risk.'

Vito's contempt for the Christmas holidays equalled his powerful work ethic which definitely wasn't what Flora was used to—though fortunately she had no trouble matching it. She'd never been a stranger to hard work. In fact, it was quite nice to feel that she'd done something worthwhile for once. Even working later than usual in the evenings became something of a pleasure, especially when she thought about all the overtime pay she was stacking up.

But it was more than that. Deep down, she rather enjoyed the mercurial company of the Italian tycoon—he was certainly a lot more interesting than Julian. And another thing—once word spread through the company that Vito was going to be around until Christmas, it had impacted onto her. His new secretary.

Suddenly, she was popular.

Flora was used to being invisible. The frumpy ex-librarian who nobody really noticed. But not anymore. Colleagues (always women) were suddenly clamouring to buy her coffee, or invite her out for drinks. Even when she refused, politely stating she would be eating her usual sandwich at her desk until after the big boss had returned to Italy, and that she didn't tend to socialise after work—that didn't seem to deter them. She was waylaid by the water cooler and confronted in the corridors, and the question they asked was always the same.

'So. What's he *like*?'

She would manufacture a close approximation of a smile before trotting out her stock answer (which she'd had to rehearse) knowing it would be extremely unprofessional to convey what she *really* felt about her boss. That Vito Monticello was utterly distracting—like a dark star which had fallen from the heavens and taken up temporary residence in the Chairman's office. They already knew that!

Or that it was difficult not to just sit there gazing at him, while forbidden fantasies strayed into her head.

Neither did she pass on that he sometimes had a very short fuse and occasionally lost his rag when women tried to ring him at the office, which they often did. These unknown females were always put through to her and Flora had strict instructions to field them, though some of the callers were very insistent. Especially that stunning model who had recently broken off her engagement to a royal prince and explained that Vito would *definitely* want to speak to her. But, mystifyingly, he didn't. She promised the woman that she would deliver a message but she was only a quarter of the way through reciting it when her boss's impatient wave of his hand cut short her words.

'Why the hell can't they take a hint?' he had demanded. 'Why do they make such doormats of themselves? If I wanted them to ring me, I would have given them my private cell phone number!'

There was, of course, no answer to that.

'He's very efficient,' Flora would say smoothly, meeting the question in yet another eager pair of eyes. 'He works from early in the morning until late in the evening.'

'He's definitely single. Right?'

Flora shrugged. 'As far as I know.'

'And he's staying at the Granchester?'

'Yes.' It wasn't breaking any kind of confidentiality code to confirm this. The fact that he was occupying the finest suite in London's premier hotel was common tabloid fodder. Someone in the post room had pointed the article out to her and suggested that even this degree of luxury might be considered slumming it for a man who was famed for having the most beautiful apartment in Milan. It had been the first and only time Flora had been tempted to access the internet and dig out what information she could about her boss.

But she had resisted. His private life was none of her business. What if she gave herself away by letting on she knew where he lived and what he liked to do in his spare time—wouldn't he rightly think she'd been *snooping*? And since such behaviour would be abhorrent to both of them, she put the thought right out of her mind and acted with nothing but cool professionalism whenever he was around. It was why she prided herself on only speaking to him when it was necessary, though at times he seemed rather bemused by her lack of engagement.

Several times she caught him watching her and once, when she'd managed to track down a file—which everyone else thought Julian might have deleted—he grudgingly bit out some uncharacteristic praise. But she simply nodded politely and rarely made small talk, even when early on she had discovered his preferred mix of coffee beans and had managed to procure a supply from a small shop in Soho.

'Mmm,' he'd remarked, his eyes narrowing with surprise. 'Nice.'

'I'm glad you approve, Vito,' she'd answered, ignoring the mocking question in his aquamarine gaze. Because didn't it give her a little rush of pleasure when she didn't conform to what he obviously expected of her? When she didn't eagerly trot out some trite explanation about contacting his Milanese headquarters to enquire about his preferred blend. It wasn't as if she was seeking praise for simply doing her job properly. Why bother him with unnecessary detail, when he had enough to do?

One dark December morning, she finished brushing out her wet hair and rode the elevator to the top of the company headquarters, to find Vito already sitting at his desk. She should have been prepared but she wasn't and as he glanced up, the unexpected reinforcement of all that raw, masculine presence at this time of the day was enough to send her heart into a dramatic thunder.

'You're early!' she accused.

His eyes glittered as he acknowledged her atypical outburst. 'But you're not.'

'No.' She didn't point out that it wasn't even eight o'clock and all the other offices were deserted. Perhaps he would like her to acquire a portable bed so she could camp down for the night and work around the clock! Still, only two days before she accompanied him to Scotland, after which Vito Monticello would be jetting off in his private jet and she doubted their paths would ever cross again. And although she told herself that was a good thing, she couldn't deny the inexplicable pang in her heart when she stopped to think about it.

She walked towards her office, acutely aware of his blue gaze following her until, just as she reached the door and the sanctity of her own little enclave, his richly accented voice stalled her.

'Flora?'

He didn't say her name very often but when he did. When he did...

Flora sucked in an unsteady breath.

It made the blood pump like mad in her veins.

It made her have the kind of X-rated thoughts which she hadn't even realised were on her radar.

Wasn't that why she had dug out these neglected clothes and given them a new lease of life? The ones she'd worn before she'd lost that bit of weight, after she'd split up with Liam. There was nothing *wrong* with them, she told herself staunchly—especially for work. Who cared that the styles were a tad dated and the length all wrong and they were a bit loose. They worked for her, didn't they? They concealed the ever-present tightening of her nipples, didn't they? She turned round and fixed her face into a pleasant smile. 'Yes, Vito?'

Vito knew he was about to break one of his rules by asking a staff member a personal question and if he was going to be here permanently, he would have resisted the temptation. But Flora Greening was a conundrum and he couldn't work out why and, as someone who liked to have all the answers at his fingertips, he found himself intrigued. He'd never met a woman like her. Not only did she never reveal anything about herself, but neither did she express a scintilla of interest in *his* life. Which was a first.

Leaning back in his chair to study her, his gaze alighted on a baggy grey skirt which came to just below the knee, teamed with a shirt which looked at least one size too big. And her hair! He realised he'd never seen it in anything other than a constricting bun, with just the occasional disobedient red-brown wave escaping from its confinement. Was it short, or was it long? He gave a mirthless smile. Who knew?

Like many of his unmarried billionaire friends cursed with the reputation of being eligible, Vito had been bracing himself for some of the more obvious ploys used by secretaries he'd worked with in the past. But for once, they had failed to materialise and his habitual cynicism had taken a severe dent. Flora Greening hadn't smartened up her appearance at all. She hadn't gone from frump to stunner overnight and started pouting at every opportunity, forcing him to request she be moved to a different department. On the contrary, her clothes seemed to have acquired an even drabber aspect than before, which was saying something.

But nobody could deny that she was an excellent worker. In fact, she was the best secretary he'd ever had, bar none. She faded into the background so that he hardly noticed she was there. Why, she was almost like part of the wallpaper! And hadn't that been refreshing after all the recent events in his life, he reflected grimly—to briefly feel as if he had found a place of refuge?

'Why do you always come to work with your hair wet?' he questioned suddenly.

She looked a little taken aback. 'Because I take a shower in the staff cloakroom.'

He frowned. 'You don't have a bathroom at home?'

Her cheeks grew red. 'Of course I do—this isn't Victorian England!'

'So?'

She shrugged. 'I cycle in every day from Ealing.'

'Ealing?' He screwed up his brow. 'Where is this?'

'West of London, sort of towards the airport. If you must know, the journey into the West End makes me very sweaty and...well, you *did* ask!' she finished, correctly interpreting his look of astonishment.

For once in his life Vito was speechless, unable to imagine any other woman of his acquaintance who would have admitted to sweating and yet for some extraordinary reason, he found her candour refreshing.

He had grown up surrounded by artifice and deception. By a hard-wired inability to accept the effects of aging and a tiresome railing against the inevitable. He thought of all the lives ruined by his mother's obsession with youth and the bitter consequences of her actions. He thought of the wiles used by so many women to try and get him to commit. And wasn't the complete absence of such wiles the reason why he felt so unusually *comfortable* around Flora Greening?

'You're right. I did ask,' he mused, twirling his gold pen between finger and thumb. 'And you cycle this long distance each day because...?'

'Oh, loads of reasons! It's economical, keeps me fit and it means I can avoid the morning crush on the Underground, which I loathe.' Her cheeks had grown pink, as if she had disclosed too much about herself. 'Er, will there be anything else, Vito?'

He put his pen down. 'Shouldn't we discuss the trip to Scotland?'

'Yes, of course. Everything is in hand,' she replied crisply, as the colour in her cheeks receded. 'We'll be flying up in your plane and there'll be a four-wheel drive waiting for us, because it's a pretty remote part of the world and the weather can be a bit dodgy.'

'I'm fully aware that we aren't headed for the great Metropolis,' he interjected dryly.

'We'll be taken to the official opening and then back to the airport the same day,' she continued smoothly. 'You'll be going off in your plane to Milan, while I fly commercial back to—'

'Ealing,' he supplied sardonically.

'Yes, Ealing. Well remembered,' she said brightly. 'I hope those arrangements meet with your satisfaction.'

'You just need to make it very clear that I must be in the air by four,' he drawled. 'I'm going skiing the next day.'

'Oh.' He could see curiosity vying with caution on

her face and curiosity won. 'You aren't spending Christmas at home?'

'No, I am not. I hate Christmas.' He met her gaze with a mocking look. 'And I like to spend it pretending it doesn't exist.'

'Oh,' she said faintly, her expression conveying that he might as well have confessed he liked ripping the wings off butterflies before her look of horror morphed into one of polite query. 'Will there be anything else, Vito?'

Vito pillowed his hands behind his head as he leaned back in the big leather chair. Yes, there most definitely was something else which would require levels of diplomacy he wasn't sure he possessed. How best to broach this, because he didn't actually want to *hurt* her?

Once again his gaze flickered over her as she stood before him with her frizzy hair and her stern grey outfit which made her look like the matron of an old-fashioned boarding school.

'You do realise that the opening of a billion-dollar wind farm is going to be a fairly formal affair?'

'Of course, I do. I'm the one who's done all the arrangements,' she said stiffly. 'Why do you ask?'

'I was just wondering what you were planning to wear?'

She chewed her lip more vigorously than usual. 'Do you always quiz your employees about their choice of wardrobe?'

'No, I don't,' he agreed, and for once his voice was almost gentle. 'But then most of my employees don't...'

'Don't...?' Her voice husked. '*What?*'

She was *not* going to force him to insult her. She was going to listen to what he had to say and absorb the truth behind the statement, as anyone else in her position would have done.

'Sometimes I think you forget that you are no longer working in the library, Flora,' he said impatiently. 'You aren't sitting behind a high counter stamping books and invisible from the waist up. You will be accompanying me and representing Verdenergia and, like it or not, people will be looking at you.' He raised his eyebrows in mocking question. 'So do you think you could possibly wear something which doesn't make you look as if you're auditioning for a part in *Les Misérables*?'

CHAPTER THREE

SNARLED UP IN all the pre-Christmas traffic, Flora bristled with fury all the way home, not in the least bit soothed by the glass of chilled white wine which Amy placed in front of her, once she had removed her waterproofs. 'How dare he speak to me like that?' she raged. 'It's an insult!'

'It's not an insult,' answered her sister patiently. 'He's only speaking the truth. He's the boss and how you look *will* reflect on him. You can scowl like mad but it won't change anything, Flora. That's how these things work.' Amy paused, before adding delicately. 'And you know, your wardrobe really could do with an overhaul.'

There was a moment of silence before Flora asked the question which was hanging in the air like a cloud. 'What's wrong with what I've got?'

There was a long pause. 'There's nothing actually *wrong* with it.' Amy appeared to be choosing her words carefully. 'It's just that you seem to have acquired this... look.'

'What sort of look?'

Her sister shrugged. 'Like you're going out of your way not to appear attractive. Almost as if you're ashamed of being a woman. You've done it for quite a while now and, yes, I know Liam hurt you, but that was ages ago.'

Flora bit back her defensive retort because deep down she knew Amy was right. Liam had been a mistake. Nothing she'd ever worn, or done, or said had been good enough. Deep down she'd known he was trying to control her but it had taken time before she'd had the courage to break away, because sometimes a relationship could feel like a refuge, even if deep down you knew it wasn't.

After they'd split it had been easier to sublimate her femininity than risk putting herself through that kind of pain again, but sometimes you could decide on a course of action and it took on a rampant life of its own. Maybe she had allowed her fear of getting hurt to turn her into someone who was becoming more and more of an outcast, who'd forgotten how to have any real fun.

'I suppose so,' she said doubtfully.

'And it seems to have got even worse lately,' Amy continued remorselessly. 'Especially since Signor Moneybags descended on the London office. What must he think about the average Englishwoman's sense of fashion? He's Italian for heaven's sake! When was the last time you bought an overcoat which didn't come from a charity shop?'

'I can't afford it,' said Flora stubbornly.

'You've got to stop thinking that way,' said Amy gently. 'I'm off your hands now, Flo. You've only got yourself to look after. Don't you realise that? You're free. Which is why I'm donating my winter wardrobe to you. And there's no point in shaking your head like a heavy-metal guitarist. I'm going to Brisbane in the New Year where the temperature is currently riding high in the thirties—and warm dresses and knee-high boots are going to be completely redundant! What's more I've got a tartan miniskirt which will be perfect for the Scottish trip. You've got a fabulous figure and you ought to show it off more often. So no more arguments. *You* are taking the lot.'

It had taken the rest of the glass of wine before Flora had reluctantly agreed. She had never known her little sister to be so bossy.

Only now, two days later, everybody in the departure lounge of the private airfield seemed to be staring at her.

Unless she was just imagining it.

No. That man who was helping himself to a croissant from the glistening heap on the fancy plate had definitely shot her a second glance. And so had the businessman on the opposite side of the lounge, next to a futuristic sculpture of a plane, who was slanting her a smile. Quickly, Flora pretended to study the blank screen of her cell phone as she waited for Vito to arrive, hating the fact that Amy's cast-offs seemed to make her so conspicuous, even if it felt refreshingly good to wear them. She had been pleasantly surprised at the image which had stared back at her from the mirror— because the tartan skirt was flattering and the soft scarlet sweater was like being coated in syrup. Even the sparkly Christmas-tree earrings were a departure from her usual sober studs, but they caught the light as she moved and made a jingly little sound which made her want to start humming carols.

She closed her eyes. She had even allowed Amy to guide her to a hair salon on Ealing Broadway where they'd chopped several inches off her hair before covering it in some gunk, so that instead of her usual waist-length frizz she now had glossy waves which tumbled to just below her shoulders. And straight after that her little sister had thrust a hastily wrapped present into her hands, telling her she'd planned to wait until Christmas to give it to her, but in the circumstances…

Some sixth sense had alerted Flora to the fact that this wasn't the usual bath bomb, or scented candle, or signed copy of a book by her favourite author. Her heart beating like a drum, she'd carefully opened it and there, cunningly hidden in the centre of a soft cashmere scarf, was a voucher from the capital's most well-known lingerie shop.

'You might as well redeem it before you go to Scotland,' Amy had declared fiercely.

And Flora had done exactly that, because wasn't the truth that she was a bit ashamed of her well-washed undies which had lost some of their elasticity? The woman in the store had been brisk and efficient as she had handed various items to Flora, who was standing behind the curtain. But when she tried on the filmy bras and marvelled at what they could do for her breasts, then slithered into high-cut briefs which had hugged her bottom, she was unprepared for her reaction.

Because all she could think about was Vito. Vito touching her, and kissing her. Heat had spiralled deep inside her, arrowing provocatively between her thighs as she imagined his golden-bronze fingers slowly peeling all the delicate garments from her body and...

'Flora?'

Given the explicit nature of her thoughts, it came as a profound shock to hear her boss's velvety voice filtering through the air and Flora's eyelids shot open to find him standing in front of her, regarding her with a look of incredulity which he made no attempt to hide. His disbelieving gaze slowly flickered from the faux-fur collar of Amy's jaunty green coat, all the way down to the soft leather boots which ended just above the knee.

She saw his features tighten—his obvious astonishment replaced by a narrow-eyed look of something she didn't recognise. Something which caused his blue eyes to grow dark and smoky and a muscle to begin an insistent beat at his temple.

As Flora stood up too quickly, the ringlety new waves bounced wildly around her shoulders and these too seemed momentarily to transfix him. But then he glared at her, which was somehow reassuring. It was certainly familiar.

'Good morning, Vito,' she said brightly.

'Good morning.' His nod was perfunctory as he gestured towards the door, and he gave a faint shudder when he noticed her Christmas earrings. 'Let's get going, shall we?' he growled. 'The plane is ready.'

For once Flora found it hard not to let her irritation show. No 'sorry I'm late', or any kind of explanation why she'd been sitting there for nearly an hour, kicking her heels. And no grudging compliment after she'd completely upgraded her wardrobe following *his* brutal assessment. Was there no pleasing the man? she wondered.

She followed him out onto the airfield where his sleek jet was waiting, wondering why he was an hour later than he'd said he would be, and why there were dark shadows underneath his eyes. He'd probably been with a woman. Up all night pleasuring someone and making her...making her...

Briefly Flora closed her eyes, willing the feelings to go away. She had to stop thinking like this. Because what if he *had* spent the night with a woman? Wouldn't it be for the best if she knew for a fact he was involved with someone—so she could kick these useless yearnings into the long grass, where they belonged? Hadn't her inconvenient crush on the Italian billionaire been growing by the day, much to her disgust? Didn't matter how often she told herself he was arrogant and unknowable, it didn't seem to change a thing. And wasn't the time to call a halt to it right now?

Obviously, she had never been on a private jet before and although the cream and gold plane was much smaller than she had imagined, it was undeniably sleek. Sliding Amy's coat from her shoulders, she waited until he had commandeered one of the squashy leather seats before positioning herself opposite him, a polished table between them.

For a moment their eyes met and it felt disturbingly claustrophobic to be sharing such a glamorous space with him. Aware of having to sit rather differently when you were wearing a tartan mini rather than a baggy skirt, Flora primly pressed her knees together.

'Have you had breakfast?' he demanded, turning his head to call for the stewardess, as if he'd rather look anywhere than at her.

'Er, not yet.'

A gorgeous stewardess appeared, nodding her immaculate brunette head as Vito spoke to her in Italian, and minutes later they were being served a veritable feast of pastries, fruit and juice, along with coffee whose delicious smell Flora recognised instantly. As the stewardess poured two cups of the steaming brew before retreating from the salon, Flora thought it felt exactly like being in a movie.

'Help yourself,' Vito suggested softly as she regarded the lavish offerings with hungry eyes.

Flora needed no second bidding. Her stomach had been rumbling with nerves about the trip since the previous evening. She was absolutely starving and these smelt so *good*. 'You aren't having any?' she questioned, biting deeply into a croissant and sighing with deep pleasure as some almond paste oozed out.

It took a couple of seconds before Vito could focus on the question because his senses were in a state of overdrive, much to his irritation. How long since he had felt such a powerful punch of lust—as if he were emerging from a dreamless sleep into bright and vivid life? Suddenly his fractured night of guilt and regret was forgotten. And even though Flora Greening was the least likely candidate to have initiated such a wild beating of his heart, wasn't he momentarily grateful that she had taken his mind off the heartbreak of his brother's death—a few short weeks after his father's demise—which hit him at times when he was least expecting it?

'No,' he answered, his throat thickening. 'I'm not... hungry.'

He was trying not to stare but where else was he supposed to look?

What the hell had *happened* to her?

Since when had his rosy-cheeked secretary decided to morph into some sort of siren?

Since he'd foolishly suggested that she might want to rethink her wardrobe choices.

He had expected her to turn up in something smart and sensible, not...

Not *this*.

He narrowed his eyes. The length of her skirt wasn't particularly controversial and was tempered by thick black tights, but the over-the-knee boots had kick-started some primitive male fantasy, as did the distracting view of her thighs. Surprisingly firm and strong thighs. Must be all that cycling, he thought unnecessarily, his mouth growing dry. She was covered from neck to waist in a red sweater which wasn't actually revealing very much. Except of course that it did, but in the most subtly provocative way imaginable. Her breasts were...

Sensational.

Full and pert and feminine. She was all firm curves and soft lines. His gaze drifted upwards, grateful that her attention was focused solely on her meal, which she was tucking into with enthusiasm, allowing him to study her unobserved.

But suddenly she lifted her head and he became aware

of the glossy ringlets which framed her face and the green-gold beauty of her eyes. Fragments of croissant were clinging to her lips and he found himself wanting to brush them away. Did he automatically touch his fingertips to his own lips, causing her to dab at the crumbs, with a self-conscious flourish of her linen napkin?

Furiously, he willed the heat in his blood to subside. It didn't matter what she wore or didn't wear. She was his secretary, for god's sake!

'When you've finished, I'd like to do some work,' he said tightly. 'It's a very short flight and there are some things we need to run through before we land.'

'Of course.' His observation seemed to have killed her appetite and her eyes were downcast as she pushed away the plate and the stewardess came in to clear the table.

He pulled a sheet of paper from his briefcase. '*Vero*. Let's run through the people I'll be meeting. Who's Hamish McDavid?'

'He's the government minister for climate action.'

'What about Angus Stewart?'

'He's the Laird whose land we rent.'

He raised his eyebrows. 'Does everyone in Scotland have a name straight out of Central Casting?'

'Is that a serious question from a man called Vito Monticello?'

He smiled.

She smiled back.

For a moment their eyes locked and Vito's hard rush of desire was superseded by an equally powerful rush of resentment. What the hell was happening here?

She wasn't his type—not in any way, shape or form.

His gaze skated over the tartan miniskirt and clinging scarlet sweater.

Except that today, maybe she was.

He shifted uncomfortably, acknowledging the heavy heat in his groin which seemed to taunt him. Yet maybe his response wasn't so surprising. Grief and guilt were powerful drivers—powerful enough to push sex to the sidelines—which was why he'd been celibate for over a year. And a man *needed* sex, he reminded himself grimly—in the same way that he needed sustenance and exercise and work. It wasn't exactly rocket science. His phone book was full of numbers of women who conformed to his chosen ideal. Beauty, brains and authority were his jam. He liked blondes who were in love with their job—mostly because it meant they wouldn't fall in love with him. He liked sex which was shallow and wild—and there were plenty of females who liked the same.

But strangely, the idea of sex as a form of physical release suddenly seemed an almost *empty* concept and Vito was glad when the plane began to descend, meaning he didn't have time to ask himself why. Beside him he heard Flora gasp as she looked out of the porthole window and he could no longer resist the temptation to look, his eyes irresistibly drawn to her.

'Ooh, look! It's snowing,' she breathed, and something in his heart twisted as he observed her almost childlike appreciation.

He followed the direction of her gaze. Illuminated by the aircraft's powerful lights, flurries of giant flakes were hurling themselves like golden arrows towards the plane's windows. 'Let's hope it doesn't get heavier and cause any unnecessary delay to my flight,' he said repressively.

He really could be a misery guts at times, thought Flora as they were whisked through airport security and into the waiting four-wheel vehicle, their passage shielded from the swirling flakes by large umbrellas held by two young women who were staring at Vito with unashamed interest. Perhaps that was the answer. Maybe he was used to constant adulation and she hadn't been paying him enough attention. Perhaps her no-small-talk strategy had backfired and that was why he was so grumpy. So chat to him. Put him in a good mood before he meets all the crofters.

'Ever been to Scotland before?' she enquired breezily, sliding onto the back seat beside him as the powerful car left the confines of the airfield and a screen silently descended, isolating them from the driver.

'Once,' he answered shortly.

'Holiday?'

'Work.' His lips twisted. 'My mother was an actress.'

'Ooh, would I have heard of her? Is she famous?'

'She's dead, but no, she wasn't famous.' His voice was harsh and, Flora thought—totally devoid of grief. 'Although she did everything in her power to make that happen.'

'How do you mean?' she asked, genuinely interested now.

The glitter of his eyes was as cold as the snowy day outside as he gestured towards the papers on his lap, his words cool and dismissive. 'What's with the sudden interrogation, Flora?' he snapped. 'Haven't you got something better you could be occupying your time with? There's plenty of work which needs my attention.'

So much for trying to get to know him a bit better. Flora fished around in her own briefcase. Fine! Who wanted to spend a two-hour journey talking to Mr Miserable, especially when it was like getting blood out of a stone? Instead, she busied herself by telephoning Hamish's secretary to check the arrangements, then stared out of the window at the falling snow, while the man across from her worked steadily, without once lifting his head.

She stared out of the window as the snowfall grew steadier. Thick clouds of flakes were tumbling down in slow motion as the car left the main road and headed towards the more desolate countryside. Soon the ancient mountains had become so blurred by white that very soon she couldn't see them at all. She was amazed that the driver could find his way, but eventually the car slowly drove up the snowy track towards the wind farm. She saw people getting out of their parked cars, rubbing their hands together and shivering beside the giant turbines as they waited for Vito to arrive.

She sneaked a glance as he got out of the car in his dark coat, the soft grey scarf around his neck making him look effortlessly elegant and very Italian. And gorgeous, she thought longingly, before she could stop herself. Tantalisingly and tauntingly gorgeous.

'*Halo agus fàilte*,' he began in Gaelic, raising his voice against the wind as the snow peppered his ebony hair and everyone clapped like crazy as he told them how happy he was to be bringing employment to the area.

Mindful of the weather, he kept it short, the Scottish minister said a few words before cutting the ribbon which flapped like crazy in the wind and, after a couple of minutes, the vast blades began to turn and everyone cheered and then began to move back towards the cars.

Vito dipped his head to hers so that she could feel the warmth of his breath on her ear. 'Now where is everyone going?'

'I told you. They've arranged a buffet lunch in the village hall followed by a ceilidh.'

'What the hell's a ceilidh?'

'Dancing. All very traditional and jolly, with lots of lovely Gaelic music.'

'Do we have to stay?'

She offered him a reproving glance. 'We definitely should. People would find it very disappointing if you didn't even put in an appearance. But of course, you're the boss,' she amended lightly. 'Nobody's forcing you. You can leave any time you like. Use the weather as an excuse—nobody will think any worse of you, I'm sure.'

'If your intention was to make me feel guilty, Flora, then you've succeeded,' he observed dryly. 'As long as I'm on that plane by four.'

'I'll make sure of it. Oh, look, the Laird's coming over to have a word with you.'

'The guy in the skirt?'

'It's a kilt.'

'Didn't I read somewhere that they don't wear anything underneath? He must be freezing.'

Flora prayed he didn't notice the instant flood of colour to her cheeks as, bizarrely, she found herself wondering what Vito Monticello would look like in a kilt. 'I really have no idea,' she said airily, as she pushed open the door to the community centre. 'But even if it's true, I think the Scots are made of stronger stuff than that.'

He gave a low laugh as he followed her inside and Flora felt another disconcerting flare of awareness because sometimes his remarks were a little too much like flirting for comfort. Did he feel he could afford to let his guard down, now that he was almost over the finishing line—and would soon be safely on his way home to Italy? It was a good thing he was leaving, she told herself firmly, so that her life could get back to something approaching normality.

Yet she couldn't help wondering what it would be like once he had gone. It was funny how you could convince yourself that because someone irritated the hell out of you—which he frequently did—you couldn't wait to see the back of them. But deep down Flora knew she was going to miss him. Vito Monticelli was a larger-than-life character. A big personality who had imprinted himself so indelibly on her life that, after two short weeks, she couldn't imagine the office without him.

She'd imagined he might find the community hall event dull and make scant attempt to hide his boredom—but the tycoon defied all her expectations. He was moving around the rather chilly space as if it were a gilded opera house and for once, his handsome features were curiously relaxed. He was chatting to the local people who had been hand-picked to meet him as easily as if he had been talking to heads of state. Flora watched, agog, as old women giggled and young lads listened to him with equal admiration. The Laird in particular seemed to be laughing uproariously at anything Vito said and Flora blinked in surprise. Who knew the Italian billionaire could be such a charmer?

The music began and she noticed the Laird hurriedly leaving the community centre—as if he had watched enough of these ceilidhs to last him a lifetime. A woman on an accordion and a man on a fiddle struck up a tune and Flora couldn't help losing herself in the music. Because hadn't music always been the thing to sustain her during the darkest times, when money had been extra-tight and she'd struggled to find treats which were free? Her tinny old radio—which she still had—had managed to come up trumps every time and she'd taught Amy the words to different songs—all their cares forgotten as they'd danced around the room, singing enthusiastically into hairbrushes masquerading as microphones. As her hips started to sway and her booted foot started tapping, Flora found herself smiling properly for the first time all day. Was it that moment of brief relaxation which made her glance up? Or some bone-deep instinct which made her realise she was being closely monitored?

Because Vito was watching her. Watching her in a way which was making her feel... She swallowed and suddenly she couldn't look away, couldn't bear to break this moment of connection—as sweet and as delicate as spun sugar. The blood rushed to her cheeks. To her breasts. Molten heat pulsed insistently inside her and Flora was grateful for a loud bang which interrupted the jollity and shattered the seductive spell Vito had cast over her.

The music stopped and everyone turned to see the door swing open, their driver stepping inside, shaking snow from his overcoat. His worried expression caused Flora to hurry across the hall and listen to his garbled words, as he explained that the heavy snowfall had effectively left them marooned.

Flora gulped. 'You're joking?'

'I wish I was, lassie.' The driver expelled a sigh, then shrugged. 'You're lucky the Laird lives so close and can offer ye a place to stay. But we need to leave now.'

'Of course,' said Flora, swallowing down her apprehension. 'We'll be right out.'

Vito's gaze remained fixed on her as she walked towards him, pushing her way through his admirers, some of whom actually glared as she penetrated the tight circle. 'Bad news, I'm afraid,' she said quietly. 'The roads are blocked.'

'So what?'

'We're going to have to stay up here for the night. The Laird has a place we can use until they can clear the snow.'

'I am *not* staying up here. Understand?' He lowered his head to hiss in her ear. 'We are travelling in a car which is built like a tank and specifically designed to cope with bad weather. And I have a flight to catch. I'm used to inclement conditions, Flora. We'll just have to take it slowly.'

'Well, you're on your own, then, because I'm not

going anywhere in this blizzard,' she retorted. 'Anyway, all your objections are academic, I'm afraid. Inverness Airport is closed.'

CHAPTER FOUR

'Is this somebody's idea of a joke?' Vito demanded from between gritted teeth, slamming the door on the swirling storm and the bright tail-lights of the car which was slowly trundling its way back up the snowy drive.

'Who's laughing?' questioned Flora sagely. She shot him a surreptitious glance. Certainly not *him*. He was glaring like mad as he shook the snow from his cashmere coat—his icy-blue eyes the only element of light in his shadowed face. 'You could have joined our driver and stayed at one of the local crofts, if this place doesn't meet with your satisfaction.'

'Don't try and be clever, Flora. I have things I'm supposed to be doing and places I'm supposed to be, namely on a skiing trip in Switzerland with friends, not stuck on some godforsaken estate in the middle of nowhere with...'

'It's Christmas, Vito,' Flora said, hugging her arms around herself to try to generate some heat, because although Amy's coat was very pretty it wasn't the warmest thing she'd ever worn. 'Most people have places to be. Even me,' she added.

But despite her reasonable tone, her heart was racing as she tried to get her head around her current reality.

She was trapped with Vito Monticello.

Stuck in a snowstorm, in the middle of nowhere with her fierce and sexy boss.

And since the glowering look he was slanting in her direction showed no sign of abating, she made another attempt to placate him, because surely it was easier going into comfort mode than allowing herself to think about the long evening ahead... 'Come on, Vito,' she said soothingly. 'Try and look on the bright side. It's not all bad.'

'You think so?' he growled.

'Of course. It was very kind of the Laird to let us stay here. I mean, obviously bad luck that his niece and her children aren't able to get here because of the snow, but a blessing in disguise for us. Believe me, there are a lot worse places to be stranded.' She glanced towards the window with a look filled more with hope than certainty. 'Who knows, they might even have the roads clear by tomorrow.'

The aristocratic landowner had described the building as a 'humble gatehouse' on the edge of his massive Scottish estate but to Flora—who was used to living in a cramped flat—it looked absolutely enormous, with a quiet and understated glamour all of its own. The beamed ceilings were high, with thick rugs scattered over honeyed wooden floors. An unlit fire sat prepared in the grate and above the marble fireplace protruded a massive stag's head whose glassy eyes were surprisingly friendly as they followed you around the room.

Landscape paintings covered every available inch of wall space and the sofas were strewn with soft blankets, all in different tartan prints. It was a warm and welcoming space—but that wasn't all it had to commend it, as far as Flora was concerned. Because, beside the huge, mullioned windows which overlooked a fairy tale landscape—stood the biggest Christmas tree she'd ever seen in a private home. Its bushy branches were covered in tiny white lights and scarlet ribbons and the whole room was scented with a fresh, conifer smell.

'The Laird is only being "kind" because my company is paying thousands to rent his land,' Vito observed acidly.

'That's a very cynical approach.'

'It might be cynical, but it's true.' He turned on her, his brow furrowing into an even more ferocious glare. 'If you think I'm happy about being holed up—'

'It's hardly a hole, Vito,' she objected. 'And we don't need to be happy all the time—grateful will do.'

'Do *not* interrupt me,' he iced back.

She met his narrow-eyed gaze. 'You were the one who told me you wanted me to be honest.'

'Which I do. But perhaps you could choose your moment before you start spouting cod psychology?' he suggested coldly, pulling his cell phone from the inside pocket of his coat. 'I'm going to ring my pilot to get his take on it. He was in the Italian air force and I'm damned sure he's navigated his way out of situations far more treacherous than this.'

'I've already told you. I'm staying put. I'm not taking any unnecessary risks.'

'Will you just be quiet and let me make this damned call?' he hissed furiously.

Flora waited in silence while he went through the pantomime of clicking on the contact, staring at the screen and then repeating the process several times until finally he gave up and hurled the phone onto the sofa, where it sank into a pile of velvet cushions.

'No signal?' she guessed.

'Top marks for observation,' came the sarcastic reply.

'I'm not personally responsible for the Artic conditions, Vito,' she snapped. 'But if you're going to stand here glaring at the Christmas tree, help yourself. Me, I'm going to explore. We're in this situation now and we have to adapt to it. We need to plan what we're going to eat and where we're going to…' The word came out as a kind of breathless gulp, which was not what she had intended at all. 'Sleep.'

His brow darkened before he gave a heavy sigh which hinted at an element of capitulation. 'I suppose so.'

To Flora's alarm and—annoyingly—her even greater excitement, Vito followed her from the sitting room as she began her silent inventory of their loaned accommodation. A quick hunt around the ground floor revealed an old-fashioned kitchen and pantry. In the centre of the scrubbed wooden table stood a fancy wicker hamper and she remembered the Laird insisting they help themselves to whatever they needed.

'So far so good,' she said, lifting up the lid and peering inside. 'At least we won't starve. There's plenty of tins in here.'

'Wonderful,' he murmured. 'The gourmet meal I was due to have in Switzerland later will pale into insignificance.'

Flora didn't respond. On one level his continued sarcasm was infuriating and yet on another, she quite welcomed the barrier it created. She *wanted* him to annoy her with his grumpiness because surely that would stop her fancying him. And she needed to stop fancying him. In the office she'd been able to keep her emotions hidden beneath the radar but that was easy when you could retreat to your own space, or sit there in your baggy clothes, diligently taking notes. But now everything had changed. Being alone with him in this picturesque lodge, wearing Amy's rather revealing tartan miniskirt, was leaving her feeling exposed in more ways than one.

Deferentially allowing him to mount the narrow stairs ahead of her, Flora knew a businesslike attitude would serve her best—otherwise Vito might conclude she was nervous about spending the night with him.

And he would be right.

But she wasn't spending the night *with* him. They might be incarcerated under the same roof but the Laird had said there were four bedrooms.

'Four bedrooms' was a bit of a misnomer. One had been repurposed as an office while a second was a repository for large pieces of furniture, covered in dustsheets. Eventually, Flora found a double bedroom and heaved a sigh of relief. The big brass bed was covered with a hand-crocheted quilt and a flower-sprigged basin and jug stood on the nightstand beside it. It was a solid and traditional room and she wondered how many generations might have used this antique bed.

Lingering on the threshold, she imagined what these four walls must have witnessed. Married couples consummating their vows, and children being born. It suggested a sense of family and continuity. Everything she'd never really had and probably never would. Amy would have them, but on the other side of the world. How often would she get to see any little nieces or nephews? she wondered, her heart clenching with pain.

She turned away, so overcome with emotion that she cannoned straight into the man who was standing behind her, and it was like colliding with a solid wall of muscle. Like soft cream meeting brittle toffee. She swayed as their bodies made contact and Vito automatically reached out to anchor her. As his hands rested lightly on her hips she could hear her heart beating out a wild and frantic tattoo. She stared up at him and suddenly all the breath left her lungs. Was it that lack of oxygen to her brain which made her feel so dizzy, or just the overwhelming sensation of his proximity?

They'd never even touched before—why would they?—but that hadn't stopped her wondering what it might feel like. She wanted it to be a disappointment, but it wasn't. Despite the innocence of the gesture, it felt like she'd died and gone to paradise and she couldn't seem to do a thing about her reaction. Suddenly her breasts were pushing hungrily against the soft wool of her sweater and she saw from the brief flicker of his gaze that her hardening nipples hadn't escaped him. Was that why his blue eyes had grown so smoky—his sensual lips curving into a line of provocation? Was he feeling it too? Like she would go mad if he didn't pull her even closer and bring his lips down on hers, in a hard crushing kiss which might rid her of some of this aching frustration.

'Steady, Flora,' he said softly. 'Look at a man like that and you might start giving him the wrong idea.'

Or the right idea, thought Flora—but she didn't say a word. She couldn't have spoken even if she could have thought of a suitable retort, she was in such a state of turmoil. And even though (disappointingly) he had let his hands slide from her hips, she felt as if he'd left his mark where he had touched her. As if the light caress of his fingers had penetrated the wool of her overcoat, lighting a secret flame within her.

She wanted him, she realised weakly. She had wanted him from the first moment she'd set eyes on him. When he'd arrived at the office like a dark and brilliant star which had tumbled straight from the heavens. Every day since then she had wanted him more—he had managed to feed her hopeless hunger for him without even trying. By now she should have become immune to his potent presence, but somehow she had not. Her unsophisticated heart still beat up a storm whenever she saw him and her stupid body reacted in a way which was unfathomable.

'What's wrong?' he prompted, regarding her with a mocking elevation of his brows, and Flora realised she was in danger of making a total fool of herself. Unless she really imagined a man of Vito's calibre would look twice at her! Talk about getting carried away with herself, or did she think she'd inherited some of Amy's glamour, along with her wardrobe?

Taking a step back, she tried to pretend that nothing

had happened. Because nothing *had*. 'Nothing's wrong,' she answered briskly. 'I'm just keen to explore the rest of this place and try to warm it up.'

His expression suggested he didn't believe her and now Flora was conscious of her boss's proximity like never before. She scooted along the narrow corridor to find another smaller bedroom but her offer to have this one died on her lips as she pushed open the door. At the foot of each narrow single bed was a Christmas stocking, spilling over with walnuts and tangerines and shiny golden coins. There was special bed-linen too—pillowcases and duvets covered with images of Santa and his sleigh. On the floor in front of the empty fire grate was a plate, upon which lay a carrot and mince pie.

'We can't use this room,' she said flatly.

'You mean because the beds are obviously designed for hamsters?'

'They're designed for *children*, Vito. And since it's obviously all set up for the Laird's niece's children and they might still get here if the airport opens tomorrow, I think we should leave well alone. But don't worry,' she amended quickly. 'I can have the sofa.'

'No, Flora,' he said, with an impatient shake of his head. '*I'll* have the sofa. I'm not that much of a brute.'

There was a pause. She could feel her cheeks growing red. 'If you say so,' she said, staring fixedly down at her boots.

As she lifted her gaze to his, unexpectedly Vito began to laugh and the unfamiliar sound shattered some of the tension simmering between them. But just as quickly the amusement vanished and his features assumed their mask of stone.

'But right now, I need a drink,' he snapped.

Nodding, she turned away. 'I'll make some tea.'

Had she deliberately misunderstood him? Vito wondered frustratedly, as he followed her downstairs, taking care to veer off in a different direction as she headed towards the kitchen, unwilling to torture himself any more by watching the sway of her delicious bottom. He'd wanted some hundred-year-old whisky, not tea. Something to relax him. To rid him of this sudden inconvenient desire for her, which had been ignited by a touch of almost laughable innocence and yet was manifesting itself in this hard and urgent aching at his groin.

And she had wanted him too. He was experienced enough to realise that there had been a connection and even as he thought about it, he felt himself getting harder. But having sex with his secretary would be a bad idea, even if—strictly speaking—she was no longer his secretary. He never blurred social boundaries by getting intimate with a staff member.

He swallowed, trying to focus on her negative traits, instead of her soft curves and trembling lips. Telling him what he needed to drink instead of asking him what he wanted. Was she now going to do that thing which all women seemed to possess at their beating heart—trying to badger him into doing what *she* wanted?

He went back into the sitting room and glared at the Christmas tree.

Trying to *control* him.

Well, good luck with that, he thought grimly. But as

he removed his cashmere coat and slung it over a nearby sofa, his simmering frustration showed no signs of abating. He was someone who rarely sat still and was always powered by pure adrenaline. Who filled every waking moment with activity in one form or another, because that was the way he dealt with life. But his briefcase was still on the plane and there was no phone signal. Nothing for his restless mind and body to focus on other than forbidden thoughts about his secretary.

At least the icy temperature stirred him into action. He found a box of matches, lit the scrunched-up newspaper beneath the pyramid of logs in the grate and soon a fire was roaring, filling the room with warmth and heat. Sitting back on his heels, he regarded his handiwork, unable to remember the last time he'd done something as basic as this. For a few seconds he allowed himself the primitive satisfaction of watching the thundering flames, when he heard the chink of china behind him and glanced up to see Flora standing there, carrying a loaded tray. The firelight was splashing her curls with copper and she had removed her green coat. In her clinging scarlet sweater and tiny skirt, there was something so intensely feminine about her that Vito forgot his irritation and acted purely on instinct.

He rose to his feet to relieve her of the tray. 'Here. Let me,' he said. 'Go over there and sit down by the fire.'

'Thanks.' But she seemed nervous as she perched on the edge of one of the velvet sofas and tried to object when he started pouring the tea.

'Why don't you let me do it?'

'What's the matter, Flora?' He raised his brows in

mocking question. 'You think I'm incapable of such a simple task?'

'I don't imagine domesticity being high on your to-do list, no.' She took the cup he handed her and shot him a curious look. 'I expect you have people to cater to your every need.'

'*Si*. I do. Aren't I lucky?' he questioned sardonically. It had always been that way. He couldn't remember any differently. There had always been an army of people employed to keep his life running smoothly. First through his parents and after that, through his own endeavours. People who cleaned his luxury apartment and Tuscan castle and cooked him gourmet meals, any time he required them. People who drove his top-of-the-range planes and cars, who fixed them when they broke, or replaced them when they were scarcely more than a year old. People who knew his measurements, who provided him with the finest handmade suits and shirts and shoes, without him ever having to set foot inside a shop. He consumed only the best the world had to offer and was protected within the privileged bubble of his billionaire lifestyle.

But sometimes that bubble felt lonely, he realised suddenly. And the last year had been as lonely as hell. The dark void left by his father's and brother's deaths had created a vacuum and into that vacuum had flooded the bitter memories and painful emotions he'd spent years trying to suppress.

'Is something wrong, Vito?'

Her gentle voice snapping him out of his reverie, Vito found her green-gold eyes fixed on him watchfully. 'You mean, other than the fact that I'm stuck in the middle of nowhere and have been forced to miss my flight?' he retorted.

She shook her head, as if determined not to react to his short fuse. 'Your face. It just looked…'

Instinctively, he tensed. 'What?'

Did his tone warn her off? Was that why she scrambled to her feet and shrugged. 'Doesn't matter. I'll take my tea with me and see what I can find for supper.'

He watched her go, allowing himself the brief, guilty pleasure of studying her compact curves before tearing his gaze away and trying to convince himself it was better when she was out of sight. Why torture himself with fantasies of the forbidden?

He threw another log on the fire and looked out of the window, where the snow was still falling in slow motion. It was, he conceded reluctantly, very beautiful and very peaceful. For once, the rest of the world and all its troubles seemed a long way away and the only sounds Vito could hear were the beating of his own heart and the spitting of the fire. And somehow those things soothed him. He yawned. Even the Christmas tree, towering over the room like a monstrous green monolith, was exuding the soft coniferous smell of the forest. As a long breath escaped from his lungs, he closed his eyes.

And slept.

When he woke, Vito wasn't sure where he was, only that it was warm and comfortable and the beating of his heart was much slower than before. He opened his eyes and yawned. Of course. He was marooned in a snowy lodge with his secretary—his escape to Switzerland postponed and his holiday plans put on hold. As someone who loathed being the victim of events outside his control, his current situation should have been enough to rile him. Yet his restlessness seemed to have fled—banished by an unheard-of nap. He glanced at his watch and gave a start of surprise. He'd been asleep for almost *two hours*. And since there was no point in reaching for his cell phone, he threw another log on the fire and went in search of Flora.

He could hear a faint crashing in the distance and followed the sound towards the kitchen, his nostrils flaring as he inhaled the scent of something unfamiliar and delicious. And there was Flora, cooking—looking unfamiliar and delicious herself.

For a moment he just stood there watching her. She had her back to him and was stirring a pot, while whistling something beneath her breath and he remembered the way she'd briefly relaxed during the ceilidh, her cheeks bright and her eyes shining—the tapping of her foot drawing his unwilling attention to her shapely thighs. Was it the bizarre circumstances in which he now found himself that had him observing the kind of everyday domesticity he had firmly banned from his own life?

Past partners had objected to his strict demands, but he didn't care. He'd learnt the bitter folly of trying to live by other people's rules and now he lived the way he wanted, without exception. Whenever he had found himself in one of the brief relationships which the press delighted in describing as *rare* (inevitably accompanied by the words *commitment-phobe*), Vito had a set of demands, which he insisted be adhered to. One was his aversion to being cooked for at home, having realised early on that allowing women into your kitchen was more dangerous than letting them get their hands on his credit card. His mouth hardened with instinctive scorn. Why believe the foolish adage that the way to a man's heart was through his stomach? Didn't they realise that he had no 'heart'—certainly not in the romantic sense. He had no intention of going down the traditional route of weddings, or babies. His determination to avoid the cloying intimacy of domesticity occasionally provoked sulking, or failed attempts to seduce him into changing his mind, but Vito always remained unwavering in his resolve.

But it seemed that here he had no choice...

He was stuck with a woman who was tempting him in all kinds of unsuitable ways and she was *cooking* for him.

The whistling stopped. She must have heard him, because she turned round—very slowly—as if she were composing herself before she faced him.

Her cheeks were flushed from cooking and her green-gold eyes looked very bright, but he noticed that her lips were pressed together, and tense. 'You're awake,' she said carefully.

'I see your observational skills haven't deserted you,' he noted.

The lips tightened into a rosebud shape. 'And obviously your sleep hasn't improved your sense of humour.'

'I wasn't aware that my sense of humour needed any

improvement,' he murmured, suddenly aware that it was a long time since he had eaten. 'What are you cooking?'

Flora was tempted to tell him *arsenic*, or sheep's brains, but since he was still technically her boss—though not for much longer—she knew she mustn't overstep the mark, just because he was making her feel churned-up. Because he was. Big time. And she had only herself to blame.

When he had fallen into that deep sleep (she had been astonished that a workaholic like Vito Monticello was able to relax so instantly)—hadn't she crept back to the sitting room to ask him some trifling question about his preferred choice of cheese? His long legs had been sprawled out in front of him, his head resting against one of the sofas and he had been out for the count. And so she had stood in the doorway, just watching him. Thinking that he looked like a beautiful, fallen angel—with his black hair gilded by the firelight and those dark lashes shielding the ice-blue glitter of his eyes. In repose his face had appeared uncharacteristically soft. Almost *touchable*. The tension around the lips had been ironed out, drawing her attention to their curved and provocative sensuality. He had looked utterly beguiling and Flora had experienced a crazy desire to go over and kiss him, as if she were in some role-reversal fairy tale and could wake him from his slumber.

She'd stopped herself, of course—imagining all too easily the horror on his face if he'd woken up to find Flora Greening drifting her lips all over his sculpted features!

'Soup,' she declared solidly. 'I found some vegetables

in the pantry and some pearl barley, so I've made us a thick broth. And there's no need to look so appalled. We have to face facts, Vito, and we really don't know how long we'll be here, do we? Or when we might next get some fresh food.'

'How practical you are,' he observed mockingly.

No, I'm not, she thought, as his gaze slammed into hers and she removed the pot from the heat. *My mouth might be saying the words I know are expected of me, but my head and my body are wishing you'd come over here and put your hand on my hips again. What is happening to me?*

'Perhaps you would like to lay the table?' she questioned.

'Lay the table?' he questioned blankly.

Despite everything, Flora smiled because he really could look very endearing. 'You never have to do that for yourself, I suppose?'

'Should I be repentant?'

'I'm not the voice of your conscience,' she answered crisply. 'And it's probably quicker if I do it myself.'

Grabbing cutlery and napkins, she ladled the soup into two bowls and put everything on the table, sliding into the seat opposite and preparing herself for some disparaging remarks about her very basic cooking. But to her surprise, Vito appeared to enjoy the rustic soup she'd prepared. He even accepted a second bowl to accompany the cheese and crackers she'd found—and there was no doubt that the warm food helped her relax a little.

But only a little.

She was still dangerously aware of his presence,

wishing her nipples would stop tightening whenever he so much as looked at her. Wishing the molten ache so distractingly low in her belly would just *go away*.

She resisted the urge to look at her watch.

How the hell was she going to make it through until morning?

CHAPTER FIVE

'So now what?'

Vito's cool question sliced through the air, shattering Flora's tranquil mood. She had been basking in a surprising contentment which had somehow crept up on her, defying her gloomy expectations. Despite being marooned in the snow with her grouchy boss, the evening had progressed more satisfactorily than she would have imagined.

Vito had suggested opening one of the bottles of red wine reposing in the hamper and she had agreed. Halfway through her first glass she had told him truthfully it was the best wine she'd ever drunk, and he had smiled in a way which made her wonder if he thought her naive. Probably. Because she was, wasn't she? Certainly compared to a sophisticated man of the world like him. And now they were sitting on the floor in front of the blazing fire with the gorgeous dark green tree glowing in the corner, while snow continued to fall outside the mullioned windows. It looked—and felt—perfect, but one look at his hard and shadowed features told her that Vito Monticello wasn't sharing the vibe. He was clearly restless, and it was a long time until bedtime.

She shifted her bottom on the rug.

Hours, in fact.

'There's not a lot on offer.' Shaking off her lethargy and morphing into her usual practical self, she shot a glance towards the window. 'We can't go outside—obviously. There's no telly or radio, and we can't even watch a film on our phones because there's no signal.'

'I never watch films on my phone,' he informed her repressively.

'Well, that's one thing you won't miss, then, isn't it?' she remarked cheerfully. 'I had a good look around while you were asleep and the good news is that I discovered two brand new toothbrushes and some strawberry toothpaste.'

'Strawberry toothpaste?' he demanded, with a shudder of distaste.

'It's obviously been bought for the children, but it's better than nothing.' She brushed a fleck of dust from her skirt. 'But unfortunately, I couldn't find any board games.'

'I'd rather not get any more bored than I already am,' he growled.

'I meant B-O-A-R-D, not B-O-R-E-D,' she spelt out laboriously, until she realised from the faint glint in his eyes that his English was easily as good as hers and he was teasing her. And she wanted to tell him not to do that. Not to do anything else which was going to make this spuriously intimate scene any more appealing than it already was. Because how long was it since she'd been in a one-to-one situation with a man like this? Too long. And never with a man like *this*. The firelight playing on his aristocratic features and handmade suit seemed completely incompatible with the rustic setting—reminding her that neither of them had a change of clothes. Not even a pair of pants, she thought worriedly. Flora swallowed. No wonder she was feeling out of her depth.

'That's hilarious, Vito. Maybe you should try a career in comedy,' she said flippantly before shrugging her shoulders. 'Well, what do you suggest we do instead?'

No other woman in this situation would have asked such a guileless question, Vito thought impatiently. Not unless they were hoping to escalate the sexual tension which was already sizzing between them. Was she? He leaned back against the armchair to study her, wondering if she had any idea of her current allure. He thought not. She might have totally transformed her appearance but there remained a peculiarly *modest* air about her, and since modesty was another quality he was unfamiliar with, it inevitably intrigued him. Just like he was intrigued by her particular blend of diffidence and boldness, meaning he was never sure which side of her would emerge. Even when she was being appropriately subservient, there was often a trace of defiance on her lips which left him feeling there was more to Flora Greening than met the eye.

His gaze swept over her and some of his habitual cynicism leeched away. She had removed her boots so he could see the outline of her slender feet and as she wriggled her toes, he wondered how on earth she could make a pair of thick black tights seem so erotic. Or was it just the powerful rush of his long-neglected hormones—reminding him of the sweet torment of desire and the way she'd responded to him when she'd bumped into him upstairs.

Did she still want him to kiss her? he wondered achingly, remembering the darkened look of appeal in her extraordinary eyes, before pushing the thought firmly from his mind. She was a complication he didn't need. A temptation which was strictly out of bounds. So why not endure some more tedious small talk until he could reasonably send her upstairs, while he tossed and turned on the sofa and prayed that morning would come quickly.

'Where were you supposed to be tonight?' he said.

'At home.'

'Partying?'

'Gosh, no.' She gave a self-conscious laugh. 'Doing last-minute prep for Christmas with my sister and her fiancé.'

She looked at him from between narrowed eyes, as if gauging the suitability of continuing and since he was—literally—a captive audience, he gave her a brief nod of encouragement.

'She's getting married in the New Year. To a doctor, actually, and then they're…they're going off to live in Australia.'

He absorbed this, heard her pride and her pain, and surprised himself by asking, 'You will miss her, I think?'

'Of course I will miss her,' she said instantly. 'What about you? Do you have any siblings?'

There was a pause. 'A brother,' he said flatly and then forced himself to say it, to try to wrap his head around what he still couldn't quite believe, even after this last long year. 'He's dead.'

'Oh, Vito. I'm so sorry. I didn't realise—'

'It's okay,' he said roughly and took another mouthful of wine. She was looking at him expectantly but he didn't elaborate and she didn't ask him to. And something about her consideration made him contemplate the unthinkable. Should he tell her that Alessandro had died, by his own hand? Should he share the unbearable weight of his brother's suicide with her?

And then what?

Pain and the inevitable guilt lanced through his heart. Sit back and wait for the rush of meaningless sympathy? Because sympathy could be a double-edged sword. It could make the person expressing it feel as if they were especially close to you and Vito had chosen never to be close to anyone.

Did she sense his sudden unease? Was that why she began to fill the silence with a nervous rush of words and complete change of subject?

'These are my sister's clothes,' she informed him chattily, gesturing towards the red-and-green skirt which had captured so much of his unwilling attention today. 'She certainly won't need them in Brisbane.'

Relieved to be distracted from the painful stab of his thoughts by such a delightful subject, Vito narrowed his eyes. 'Hence the sudden and rather surprising transformation,' he observed slowly.

'Well, you were the one who suggested I smarten up before our trip here!'

'So I did,' he agreed. 'I just wasn't expecting something quite so…'

'So what?' she questioned, sounding even more defensive now. 'Go on, Vito—you can speak freely.'

'Dramatic,' he concluded.

'I don't know what that actually means. Is it a euphemism for me looking like mutton dressed up as lamb?'

He narrowed his eyes. 'Excuse me?'

'A woman who's wearing clothes which are too young for her,' she explained, self-consciously tucking one glossy wave of hair behind her ear. 'You strike me as a man of the world—'

'Is that what you think of me?' he said mockingly.

She shrugged. 'Kind of. So if you think my outfit is too revealing, or I'm too old to carry off a skirt like this, it might be helpful to know.'

Aware that he was now entering dangerous territory, Vito didn't answer immediately, because a woman who was seeking reassurance was often seeking something else. But suddenly he found himself wanting to wipe all that doubt and uncertainty from her lovely face. 'I think you look hot,' he informed her frankly.

'Hot?' she questioned in alarm.

Had something been lost in translation? he wondered. 'Like a young woman in the very bloom of her life,' he elaborated, seeing her look of surprise. 'Which makes me wonder why you usually dress as if you're trying to hide from something,' he concluded softly.

Something? Flora thought dazedly. Or someone? Still reeling from his lavish praise, she considered his question. She wanted to tell him it was none of his business—which was true—but the reason she was reluctant to answer was more damning than that. She remembered the way Liam had rounded on her, had called her frigid and unimaginative, and no way was she admitting to *that*.

'I had a bad experience,' she said evasively.

'A man?' he guessed.

Flora nodded, and something about the perception gleaming from his eyes made her ask tentatively. 'How did you guess?'

'It's not exactly rocket science,' he said bitterly. 'Men and women have a habit of trying to destroy each other.'

Perhaps it was the bleakness in his voice which made Flora realise he wasn't entirely immune to pain himself. Was that why she started to confide in him—Vito Monticello, of all people? 'He kind of wrecked my confidence when I said I didn't want to marry him,' she said slowly.

'You shouldn't have let him have that power over you,' he observed.

'You think?' Flora gave a short laugh. 'Sometimes that's easier said than done. I'm not much of a game-player,' she admitted. 'So I decided that life was easier without the complications of men and I got into the habit of dressing in such a way that made it clear I wasn't putting myself out there.'

He absorbed this in silence and nodded, running a slow thumb over the shadow of his jaw. 'A habit which perhaps became a little more pronounced after I arrived?' he suggested, after a moment.

He *knows*, Flora realised, with a sudden wash of shame. For all her supposedly determined efforts to keep her feelings beneath the radar, had Vito Monticello been aware of her lust for him all along? Perhaps this was an occupational hazard where he was concerned. Did he sit back and witness countless foolish secretaries losing their hearts to him? Did he think she'd *deliberately* cannoned into him upstairs, hoping for a kiss?

'What do you want me to say, Vito?' she questioned, in a low voice. 'That I fancied you like mad and was terrified of how vulnerable that made me feel at work?'

There was a pause. 'Only if it's true.'

She wanted to deny his silken suggestion. To maybe give a short laugh and tell him he was out of his mind. But she wasn't the kind of woman who could carry off such a barefaced lie and besides, indignation was in short supply when confronted by the smoky smoulder of his gaze, which was setting her blood on fire. And what was the worst that could happen if she admitted it? Since he was the one probing for an answer, he could hardly accuse her of insubordination if she answered him honestly. The much more likely scenario was that he'd reassure her, telling her he would regard it as nothing more than a sweet and rather naive compliment and they would never speak of it again.

'Yes, it's true!' she said, with a fervour which seemed to rush from her lips of its own accord, before lifting a defiant chin. 'Satisfied?'

'*Satisfied?*' He gave an odd laugh. 'Oh, Flora. Did you choose that word to taunt me, knowing that the only thing which would satisfy me right now would be if I were to lie you down on that rug and start making love to you?'

Flora's hand fluttered to her sternum, her fingertips

colliding with the soft, red wool as she stared at him in confusion. 'Is that some sort of joke?'

'Do you really think I've been immune to you all this time?' he demanded unsteadily. 'That it was only your short skirt and clingy sweater which turned me on—that I am like a magpie, only attracted to something shiny?' He paused. 'Surely you must realise that the imagination can be the most powerful aphrodisiac of all, which is why your dowdy attire failed to do its job properly.'

'D-did it?'

He shrugged. 'Frankly, I get bored by the amount of flesh I see on display these days. I know it's a deeply unfashionable view, but I find it vulgar. Don't you realise that modesty can be unbearably tantalising? That what you can't see can be even more enticing than what you can? I didn't imagine the chemistry we shared a couple of hours ago, and neither did you.' His voice dipped into a velvety caress. 'It was so innocent and yet so damned...*hot* that it was almost combustible. What's the matter, Flora? Why are you staring at me like that? Do you consider yourself so undesirable that you don't believe what I'm saying?'

I know I'm undesirable, she wanted to tell him miserably, yet somehow the way he was looking at her was managing to contradict all her old beliefs. She could feel her body silently responding to his words and for a moment she allowed herself to revel in this alluring and entirely unexpected reinforcement of her own sexuality. But that was dangerous. She stared down at the fingers which were clasped together in her lap, not daring to speak nor even to move, unsure of where this was going.

And that was dangerous too.

'Flora?'

She lifted her head, acknowledging the dark melt of his eyes and her heart turned over with lust and longing. 'What?' she whispered.

'We could spend hours skating around the subject, or we could cut to the chase.'

She nodded. 'Go on, then,' she said cautiously.

'Do you want me?'

Her mind was working frantically, trying to fight with her body—and her mind was losing. 'You know I do,' she said in a low voice. 'But you're my boss.'

'But I'm not. Not anymore. Dante Antonelli will be arriving after the holidays and you told me yourself that you intend to look for a new job.' There was a pause as he shot her a look of soft challenge. 'So if that's your *only* objection…'

It wasn't, of course—there were others. Flora stared into his beautiful face. He was about as far out of her reach as the cold stars in the sky above. Their worlds were poles apart. She was an ordinary woman from West London who just about managed to make ends meet—not a model, or an actress, or a high-powered businesswoman, who were undoubtedly his more usual type of bed partner.

But more than any of these things, she just didn't know much about men. She'd hardly been able to deal with Liam—who was a painter and decorator from West London—let alone a powerful billionaire who jetted around the world on his private jet.

This shouldn't be happening and there was a bit of

her which didn't really believe it was. Yet the reality was that Vito Monticello wanted to get intimate with her and the idea didn't seem a bit outrageous. Was that because they were stuck in this picturesque lodge with thick snow outside—with the added magic of Christmas thrumming away in the background—which made such an idea seem so *normal*?

But it was risk all the same, and risk was something Flora had avoided, ever since those grim-faced police officers had knocked on her door all those years ago to tell her that Mum was gone. When she had vowed that nothing or no one, was ever going to hurt her like that again.

So she had played safe.

With Liam.

With everything.

The thrift-shop clothes and the homemade sandwiches. The money she still squirreled away in case Amy might one day need it. She'd denied herself stuff for so long that she did it automatically and convinced herself she didn't mind. And mostly she didn't. But...

Couldn't she do something for herself for a change?

Why the hell not?

Stretching her legs out in front of her she saw Vito's eyes following the movement almost helplessly and Flora was filled with a sudden rush of elation as she saw the expression on his face. She wanted to remember this moment, when this gorgeous, powerful man had looked at her with hunger darkening his icy eyes. She wanted to bury it deep inside her mind so that she could drag it out like a glittering treasure on dark and drizzly days and study it.

'No, it's not my only objection,' she conceded, in a voice which didn't sound like her voice at all. Just like her body didn't feel like her body as she leaned back on her elbows, the movement automatically thrusting her breasts forward in silent invitation, as if she'd just received a crash course in provocation. 'But I'm prepared to overlook the rest, if you are.'

He made a sound at the back of his throat, midway between a growl and a laugh. It was primitive and triumphant and seemed to set down invisible markers, which Flora knew she'd be a fool to ignore. The earthy sound drove home the fact that this was sex—and nothing more than sex. But who cared when he was moving towards her like that, his eyes flashing dark fire as he reached her and captured her face between his palms.

'But we need to be clear on something, Flora,' he stated huskily, as he stared down at her.

'What?' she whispered distractedly, wishing he would just *kiss* her.

'I want you. Very, very much. But what I don't want are any regrets or recriminations. This is for one night, and one night only.'

'Like the circus, you mean?' she questioned flippantly.

His thumb grazed the outline of her trembling lips, which opened instantly beneath his touch. 'Do you understand?' he demanded urgently.

'Yes, *yes*!' she said, trying to convince herself that she should be grateful for his candour. Of *course* it was only going to be one night—and she told herself that was a good thing. A liberating thing, meaning she could be as wild as she liked. Because suddenly she was feeling *really wild*, which also wasn't like her. She swallowed. Not like her at all. 'Just kiss me,' she urged.

'My pleasure,' he murmured, and lowered his head to hers.

She'd thought it would be a hard and masterful demonstration of power, but she was wrong. Flora moaned, because who knew a kiss could be this slow? Especially when delivered by a man known for his impatience. But it was as though Vito Monticello had decided he had all the time in the world, or maybe he was just demonstrating his steely sense of control.

He kissed her until she was soft with longing, until she tightened her arms around his neck and her breasts started pressing against the hard wall of his chest. And then the kiss got deeper. Seeking. More urgent than before.

Flora trembled as he pushed her down onto the thick sheepskin, realising he was going to do it to her *here*, in front of the fire and the Christmas tree. And something about the way he was looking at her and the way he was touching her was turning her on even more. He was taking off her clothes as if he wanted to see her properly, rather than hiding her away beneath a duvet. Could it get any more fantastic? she wondered dazedly.

The answer was yes. Much more. Especially when he peeled her sweater over her head.

'Wow,' he murmured, his eyes narrowing with smoky

appreciation when he clocked her new bra. 'Your breasts are incredible.'

'Are they?'

'You know damned well they are,' he growled.

Well, she didn't actually—but she was willing to be convinced, especially when he was using his mouth on them like that. Flora tipped her head back as he flicked his tongue over the delicate lace, when an anxious thought was enough to halt her rapidly escalating rapture.

'V-Vito?'

He lifted his head from her breast and she could see a muscle working at his cheek. 'You want to change your mind?' he gritted out.

'God, no. It's just...'

'Just what?' he prompted, the relief in his tone evident as he focused on pulling off her thick tights.

Flora swallowed as she lifted her bottom to help him. 'You do realise these are the only clothes we've got?'

'Well, I'm not about to rip these panties off if that's what you're worried about.' His eyes narrowed appreciatively. 'Especially as they are such exceptionally pretty panties.'

'Thank you,' she said, offering up a silent prayer of thanks to Amy for her perceptive early Christmas present. 'But that's not what I meant. You've got more clothes on the plane but I haven't and I—'

'You don't have to stay in organisational mode all the time,' he reproved, slithering the filmy briefs down over her thighs and dropping them to the floor. 'None of your concerns will be a problem. There will be fresh clothes available when we are rescued.'

'Because in your world everything can be solved by the snapping of your fingers?'

'Something like that,' he conceded, though a note of impatience had entered his voice. 'So why don't you stop worrying about logistics and undress me instead?'

Did he think her passive? Flora fretted, as she began to comply. Would her fumbling fingers betray her inexperience of dealing with a handmade suit of this calibre? Pushing the expensive jacket from his shoulders, she started to unbutton his shirt, letting her palm rest on the thunder of his heart as she began to explore his hard-packed torso. As she scraped her fingernails over the silken skin, she heard his shuddered response—and didn't it thrill her that she could make this powerful man sound almost *helpless*?

She pulled off his bespoke shoes and fine socks and pushed them to one side. Next, she undid the buckle of his belt and unzipped his trousers. It should have been the most bizarre occupation in the world, peeling off her boss's silken boxers and being confronted by his huge erection—but instead it felt completely natural.

'You're beautiful,' she said, almost without thinking, as the last of his clothing was removed and his powerful body was illuminated by firelight.

'Am I?'

Flora nodded as her fingertips skated over him. He was all hard planes and honed muscle. Taut torso and flat belly, and beyond that his massive cock, standing proud against his belly—a pale pole against the richness of his olive-dark skin. Maybe she should have felt daunted by the sight of all that raw, masculine power but she didn't. She felt empowered by it. By him. By the way she seemed able to turn him on so easily. As his gaze burned into her, she felt as if he were drawing her deep inside him—as if some incredible sexual osmosis was taking place and two people were becoming one. 'Totally beautiful,' she affirmed huskily.

A faint frown creased his forehead and Flora wondered if she should dial down the praise for fear of frightening him off. Maybe. She closed her eyes as he began to touch her, not wanting him to read any vulnerability in her eyes, but soon her insecurities were eclipsed by desire as he stroked with a sureness of touch which had her quivering with anticipation.

'Do you like it when I do this?' he enquired almost carelessly, as he dipped his head to the fullness of her breasts and circled his tongue around each puckered nipple.

Her mouth was so dry she could barely get the word out. 'Y-yes.'

He drifted his hand downwards, past the soft fuzz of curls, to where she was unbelievably sensitive. Gliding one long, slow finger over her quivering core, her body almost jackknifed with pleasure and he lifted his dark head to subject her to the smoulder of his molten gaze. 'And you definitely like that,' he murmured approvingly.

Flora couldn't seem to find the words to agree, but maybe words were becoming redundant because now she was wriggling restlessly. Her hungry body was making demands which were drowning out every other consideration. Suddenly she wanted more than this skilled demonstration of how thoroughly he could turn her on—as if he were methodically going through a tick box of foreplay. Because even though she wasn't used to foreplay, it wasn't enough. She wanted him. Not *playing* with her as if he were tinkering with a car engine, but inside her. Hard and hot and deep inside her. Reassuring her that this was real and not some kind of dream.

As if he'd read her mind—or her body—he reached for his discarded jacket and removed a condom from his wallet. He glanced up as he ripped open the foil, a slow smile curving the edges of his lips.

'Do you want to take over?' he questioned, sliding the protection over the thick shaft.

'I don't think my hands are steady enough,' she told him truthfully.

Wordlessly, he moved over her and she opened her legs. His blunt tip nudged insistently against her heat and she elevated her hips in silent invitation. And then it was happening. He was easing himself inside her. Pushing deeper and deeper until he had filled her completely and along with the instant rush of pleasure came another, even more powerful sensation. It was as though she had been born with an empty space inside her, a space which had only ever been intended for Vito Monticelli and now he was inside her like this, he had made her complete. Choking out a broken cry she pressed her lips into his shoulder as she clung to him and momentarily, he stilled.

'I'm not hurting you?' he demanded.

'No!'

He tilted her head back, his gaze devouring her, scanning her trembling body as if he had never seen a naked woman before and she saw his features darken as something else must have occurred to him and he caught hold of her arms. 'Please tell me you're not a virgin,' he husked.

Which she supposed spoke volumes about her technique! Flora shook her head and felt his grip relax. She wasn't a virgin but right now she felt like one. As if this was the first time.

The only time.

And no way was she going to let him know *that*.

'No. It's just been a long time,' she reassured him quickly, brushing her lips over the strong column of his neck. 'But please don't stop.'

'You think I could?' he questioned unsteadily. 'Even if I wanted to?'

He pushed in even deeper, right up to the hilt, burying himself inside her as he took up a steady rhythm and Flora gasped. Wrapping her thighs around his back, she moaned as he drove even harder. His mouth was on her neck, her jaw and finally, her lips and as he deepened the kiss, she tangled her fingers in his hair. As his movements grew faster, she could feel the beckoning of something incredible and suddenly she felt a sense of desperation as she tried to reach it.

'Relax, *cara*,' he urged her unevenly. 'Don't try too hard.'

As she followed his husked advice, she could feel all his raw power flowing into her. The tiny tremors which had seeded in her core were now blossoming into fierce shudders of need, and Flora held her breath as her pelvis tightened and the world suddenly exploded into a sea of stars. Surge after surge of pure delight threatened to take her under and then Vito was groaning out his own pleasure, his big body shuddering as he made each choking thrust.

He stayed inside her for a long while before withdrawing and when she opened her eyes he was staring down at her, his face tight with question as his fingertip traced a wavy track on one of her cheeks.

'Tears?' he questioned softly.

Surely there was nothing wrong with admitting what had just happened, to a man who had just brought her so much pleasure, who had proved beyond any doubt that she wasn't frigid at all. 'It's...it's never happened like that for me before,' she confided shakily. 'I've never had an orgasm like that.'

He nodded, then drew her comfortably into his embrace. 'Good,' he said, almost absently, and dropped a kiss onto the top of her tangled head. 'I'll give you another one in a minute.'

CHAPTER SIX

Where *was* he?

Vito opened his eyes and blinked against the intense brightness, his eyes narrowing as he stared out of the window.

Outside the world was white and cold, while inside it was vibrant and warm.

And right here beside him was the source of all that warmth…ripe and sweet and soft.

His gaze drifted downwards, to where Flora's shiny curls were resting against his chest, her face buried against his nipple so that he could feel her even breathing against his skin, which was still damp with sweat. Unsurprisingly.

His mouth dried. If sex were a sport, they'd be in line for a gold medal. How many times had they done it? Not as many times as he would have liked, but he had been woefully underequipped. If he'd known that he was going to end his year-long bout of celibacy in such an unlikely way, he might have taken time to pack more condoms.

As the automatic jerk of yet another erection made itself evident beneath the bedclothes, he wondered whether the snow had started melting, but going over to the window to find out would wake her. And he didn't want to do that.

Not yet.

Not until he had come to terms with the crazy events of the previous night.

He gazed up at the ceiling. They'd finally made it to bed when the fire had burnt down, rushing upstairs to avoid the icy temperatures in the rest of the house and brushing their teeth with some bizarre tasting toothpaste before finally settling down in the big, brass bed for the night.

Not that there had been very much settling involved…

What had followed had been the stuff of his wildest fantasies. It just hadn't been what he'd been expecting—in any way. Flora had been eager and ready for anything, yet there had been something curiously *wholesome* about having sex with his secretary. She hadn't demonstrated a series of sophisticated sexual techniques intended to physically ensnare him. On the contrary, it had been her total lack of guile which had made that first time so incredible, though her tears had taken him by surprise.

And then she had confided in him, those long lashes fluttering down over her wet eyes. That he had been responsible for her first ever penetrative orgasm should have filled him with a swaggering kind of masculine pride, yet it had made him feel curiously protective. And cautious. Because a disclosure like that had all kinds of implications, not least that she'd felt relaxed enough to tell him. Was she imagining a special bond between them because he had given her such pleasure—

and would she let that imagination run away with itself? He didn't want her thinking he was some kind of superstud, or imagining that their one night could be extended. Because she was too sweet for a man like him. Her face had been so open and vulnerable, her lips trembling with soft joy at the discovery of how fantastic sex could be and he had felt the unwanted twist of his heart, which had concerned him.

'Vito?' she murmured sleepily.

He had been planning to get up and take a shower in that icy bathroom—not least to kill his desire—but the brush of her warm body against his was too powerful an enticement to resist. He started to kiss her, her lips automatically opening beneath his and she gasped as he deepened the kiss. Her soft curves were moulding themselves into his rocky flesh and her curls were tumbling through his hands like satin. She was still half-asleep, he realised as her eager little fingers curved possessively around the steely length of his erection and she guided him towards her waiting wetness.

'Wait,' he mumbled reluctantly as he felt the press of her silken heat. Blindly, he reached for the last condom and slid it on with difficulty and she giggled as she assisted him and that made him harder still.

Lifting her up he brought her slowly down onto his waiting cock, feeling her molten slickness as he felt that first sweet connection. And then he was properly inside her and she was as tight as he remembered. So tight, he thought hungrily—like a velvet vice. She hadn't been a virgin but she might as well have been. She was moaning softly as he moved, her lips against his ear as he made each powerful thrust and her murmured words of incitement were turning him on even more.

He could feel her body tense and change and then she made that breathless little cry he'd grown to know so well, as she began to contract around him. And something about the way she was making him feel—almost as if he were out of control—made a flicker of resentment wash over him, which was immediately obliterated by a powerful rush of desire. Somehow, he maintained his steady rhythm until he felt the last of her tiny tremors and then gave himself permission to come—shudderingly helplessly as his orgasm sucked him under and seemed to go on and on.

He wasn't sure how long it took for him to drift back to consciousness, only that when he finally opened eyelids which felt as if they'd been weighted with lead, it was to find Flora lying there, just watching him. Propped up on one elbow, her eyes were glittering, her cheeks all flushed and there was a dreamy smile of satisfaction on her lips. Had she been watching him while he slept? he wondered suspiciously—and why did that suddenly feel like an intrusion?

'Good morning!' she said softly.

Vito's heart sank as reality hit him like a sledgehammer. Oh, hell. All that sweetness and trust, so glaringly apparent in the shining of her eyes. As if he were some kind of god rather than a mere mortal. He wanted to tell her not to look at him like that. That he didn't deserve her adoration or regard. That his conscience was heavy with the weight of all that he had done—or failed to do. That he was nothing but a cold hard-hearted bastard and she would be better off forgetting all about him. She might need a little guidance with that particular strategy, he realised suddenly. He might need to give her no choice other than to forget him.

'Sleep well?' he questioned conventionally.

'Well...eventually.' Her eyes danced with conspiratorial glee as her finger located his belly-button and slowly began to inch down towards the stirring throb of yet another arousal. Vito's throat dried as he found himself growing hard again, despairing of his instant capitulation to her feathering touch. He had to call a halt to this right now. Up until yesterday she had been his secretary! And yet today she had become the instigator of the kind of desire he hadn't experienced since...

Since when?

He swallowed.

He couldn't remember.

As a teenager his libido had naturally been fierce and intense, though inevitably lacking the finesse brought about by experience. Over the years his reputation as a lover had been legendary and women had always made themselves available to him. But Vito was choosy—if he'd taken up all the offers which came his way he would have spent his life in bed. Yet his more recent sexual experiences—admittedly over a year ago now—had left him feeling distinctly jaded. Even—dare he say it—*bored*? As if he'd seen it and tried it all before. Sometimes sex had seemed more like a purposeful workout at the gym than...

What?

Hadn't there been moments when Flora Greening

had clung to him, that the world had felt like it was tilting on its axis and threatening to spin out of control?

And he needed to stop thinking that way.

He closed his eyes as he felt the purposeful tiptoeing of her fingers, resenting the spring of his erection and wanting nothing more than to flip her onto her back and push inside her again. She would love it. She would make that throaty little sound of delirious joy, which only enhanced his own fierce rush of pleasure. And he would love it too.

And that would be wrong—and not just because he was right out of condoms. He scowled. No way should he be in this position. Naked in bed with Flora Greening? *Santo cielo!* Yes, it had been spontaneous and amazing but it had also been a very stupid idea and he should have used his legendary powers of self-restraint to stop himself.

But now was not the time to compound his transgression by feasting on her body again. They had both agreed this was a one-off. And even though he suspected her agreement might have wavered this morning—judging by the way she was currently kissing the roughened shadow of his jaw—he was determined to honour the agreement they'd made. There wasn't going to be a repeat. From here on in he needed to act like nothing had happened and ultimately, he would be doing her a favour.

Removing her hand from his belly, he couldn't miss the flare of disappointment in her eyes as he leaned over to glance at his watch. 'I need to go and find out what's happening,' he said thickly, as he willed the terrible aching to subside.

'But surely the Laird will come and tell us if there's any news about the airport being cleared?'

The note of frustration in her voice was apparent and Vito's lips curved with disdain. Did she imagine he was going to spend the entire morning in bed with her—rising like some walking wreck when the guy in the skirt came to find them? 'I'm not sitting waiting around for someone else to use their initiative, Flora,' he clipped out. 'Surely you must have realised by now that I'm not that kind of man?'

Crushing the desire to feast his eyes on her flushed body, he rose quickly from the bed and went over to the mullioned window, where the scene outside resembled the set of one of those old-fashioned Hollywood movies. But the snow machine must have stopped working during the night, he thought, because not a single flake was falling from a sky coloured bright blue instead of deepest grey. The ground was coated with snow which glittered like diamonds in the sunshine and Vito was rewarded with the sight of water dripping slowly from a laden branch, on which a robin sang lustily.

'It's melting,' he said, spotting a wide space of accessible white land in the distance. '*Eccellente*,' he murmured. 'I see no reason why they won't be able to get a helicopter here.'

Flora tried to look enthusiastic as Vito turned around, his face alight with relief. He obviously couldn't *wait* to get on his way. Which was exactly how it was supposed to be, she reminded herself fiercely. He'd told her from the start that this was a one-off and she had agreed. Just because he had shown her she was capable of giving and receiving more pleasure than she'd ever thought possible, that didn't change anything. What did she think was going to happen? He wasn't going to suddenly ask her to Milan to go on a date, or to join him on his ski trip!

It was time to step up to the plate and play the part expected of her. Not the writhing sensual Flora of last night but his usual sensible secretary who was prepared to forget her brief indiscretion.

Let him remember you as a cheerful person and not someone who's all needy and clingy.

With a monumental effort Flora slanted him a smile, trying to ignore the fact that he was completely naked, determined to make some normal-sounding conversation before they went their separate ways. 'So who's going to be on the slopes with you?'

'Two friends from way back—Alessio Cardini and Marco Pallotta. We often go away at this time of year—usually to Gstaad—to escape from the inevitable nightmare of the holidays.'

Flora remembered when he'd arrived in London. The way he'd torn through the Verdenergia building demanding the removal of all decorations. The way he'd shuddered when he'd seen the giant conifer here in the lodge. 'Why do you hate Christmas so much?' she questioned.

'How long have you got?' His jaw tightened with contempt. 'It's nothing but a charade, maintaining the total myth of the happy family. And the whole damned world colludes.'

'There must be *some* happy families,' she said lamely.

'Not in my experience, and all the stats back it up, don't they? That's why I'm never planning to join the ranks of the majority. I don't want marriage and I don't want children,' he growled, fixing her with a piercing stare. 'What about you, Flora? Was your childhood "happy"?'

'It was...unconventional.' She shrugged. 'I didn't know my dad, and my mum died on a mountain.'

'Tough,' he said tersely. 'How come?'

'Because she was a rock climber and that was her first love.'

He narrowed his eyes. 'Selfish,' he observed.

'That's one way of looking at it. Fathers are allowed to have passions but not mothers, it seems,' Flora commented acidly. 'It was just me and Amy for a long time but I like to think we made the best of it.'

'My parents fought like cat and dog until they were divorced,' he said slowly, a note of bitterness in his voice. 'And then they fought even more, until my mother died.'

His face had suddenly darkened and as Flora automatically uttered words of sympathy for his loss, she knew him well enough to recognise that the subject was now closed. And even though she would have liked to find out more about what really made Vito Monticello tick, she accepted it was not her place to ask. She didn't want this extraordinary night to end on a bad note. She was supposed to be all grown-up and cheerful, wasn't she? *So do it!*

'Anyone else going on this ski trip?' she enquired sunnily.

'Is that a coded way of asking whether we're taking any women with us?'

'No! Well, maybe a bit,' she admitted, blushing a little as his gaze bored into her.

'Do you really think I'd have slept with you if I had another bed partner lined up for the holidays, Flora?' he demanded. 'Do you think I'm one of those men who trawls from woman to woman, who can't keep it in his trousers?'

All she'd been doing was trying to put their casual hookup in the correct pigeonhole and now he was making it sound as if she were impugning his honour!

'There's no need to be so touchy,' she said.

'I am *not* being touchy!'

For a moment they glared at each other across the traditional room and Flora found herself wondering how many other couples had rowed in this room, over the centuries.

But never in circumstances like this, she surmised as, disappointingly, he turned away and headed off towards the bathroom. And somehow she wasn't surprised when he returned a short while later, fully dressed, right down to his cashmere coat and shiny handmade shoes, which he must have retrieved from the fireside.

'I'm going up to the main house to use the phone,' he announced. 'They're bound to have some sort of signal there. I'll need to speak to my pilot about getting us out of here, and also about making sure there's a connecting flight to take you on to London. With a bit of luck, you should be back before too long.'

Flora looked at him hopefully. 'Shall I get dressed and come with you?'

'No.'

The curtness of the word echoed around the room as he picked up his watch from the nightstand and slid it onto his wrist. 'Why don't you stay here?' he suggested, his gaze encompassing the rumpled bed-linen. 'Tidy up a little maybe, hmm?'

It was probably the most insulting thing he could have said in the circumstances, and not just because he was reinforcing stereotypical roles and putting her in a subservient position, and sounding just like her boss again.

He seemed to be forgetting the fact that they were lovers. *Had* been lovers, she corrected herself as she forced herself to confront the bitter truth.

He doesn't want anyone to know what we've been doing, she recognised painfully. *I'm obviously supposed to remove any sign that two people might have spent the night here having mad, passionate sex.*

Perhaps he was worried about the sensibilities of the Laird's young niece she thought, but without any real conviction. And perhaps he was doing her a favour by reminding her of the huge divide between them, lest she have the temerity to forget that she was nothing but a humble secretary and he was the powerful boss...

That was all they were.

All they were ever intended to be.

'Sure,' she said, with an easy smile, as if she didn't really care, one way or another, and she turned away before he could see the prick of tears in her eyes. 'I'll see if I can find a pair of rubber gloves.'

CHAPTER SEVEN

THERE WERE GOLDEN crackers and sparkling tinsel and age-old carols playing on the tinny radio. The King had just finished his speech and a succulent turkey was glistening on the table, just waiting to be carved, and since Amy's fiancé was a surgeon, Flora didn't doubt for a moment that he would make a brilliant job of it.

Sitting back in her chair, she tried to appreciate the cosy scene which lay before her, thinking it was about as Christmassy as anyone could ask for. Who cared that the tiny tree in the corner was about a tenth of the size of the one which had dominated the snowy lodge in Scotland, or that the windows of the Ealing flat badly needed replacing and the wind was whistling in through the odd crack? Amy and Brett had organised absolutely everything and when she'd arrived back from Scotland, she hadn't had to lift a finger.

So why wasn't she feeling a bit more gratitude?

Why was she feeling so *weird*?

Because she was missing Vito like mad, despite all her best intentions to put him out of her mind?

How stupid was that?

Their departure from Scotland had gone as smoothly

as clockwork. Refusing to get into a sulk about her boss's chauvinistic allocation of chores, Flora had cleaned the lodge so that it sparkled. She'd even gone out and picked some sprigs of holly to display in a brass bowl on the kitchen table—and the last thing she'd heard was that the Laird's niece and her children were en route, in time for the big day. At least that was *something* to cheer her heart. She had even taken a big bite out of the stale mince pie from the plate in front of the fireplace, to make it look as if Santa had made good his promise to come down the chimney.

A helicopter had been dispatched to take her and Vito to the airport and there they had parted company— the billionaire leaving on his private jet to Gstaad, while Flora had taken a scheduled flight to Heathrow. She had lifted her face to his—more in hope than in expectation—but there had been no longed-for kiss, only a brief touch of his leather-gloved hand to her cheek and a murmured entreaty to take care of herself.

'I'm sure you'll get on with your new boss,' he had added, and for a moment she had blinked at him in surprise, suspicious about what he meant by that. Surely he wasn't suggesting that she was one of those secretaries who put out for *everyone* she worked for? Refusing to allow herself to fall down the neurotic rabbit hole of worrying about other people's expectations, Flora had managed to produce a cool and non-committal smile in response.

'Oh, I'm sure I will,' she had agreed airily.

He had given her a brief nod and walked away and she

had quickly turned her back, refusing to watch him leave for fear she might reveal her ridiculous sense of sadness.

Flora didn't know who had arranged her journey back to London, only that she had been upgraded to the front of the plane. But the flight was too short to make the most of the freebies on offer and for some reason her stomach had lurched when the stewardess offered her champagne. Even the bright Christmassy lights of the capital had failed to lift her flagging spirits and neither had the brass band playing lustily outside Ealing Broadway station, as she had stuffed a crumpled note into their collection tin.

And now she was mechanically working her way through a turkey dinner she would rather have avoided but didn't dare refuse, for fear it would arouse her sister's suspicion. Heaven only knew but Amy was being suspicious enough already and she hadn't eased up on her interrogation.

'So, you're telling me you spent the night *alone* in some remote lodge place with the hot billionaire?'

'There's no need to make it sound like that,' said Flora crossly, sawing her way through a Brussels sprout.

'Like what?' questioned Amy, all faux innocence. 'You can't blame me for being interested when you came back looking like...'

Flora put her fork down as her sister's words tailed off. 'Looking like *what*?'

Too late she realised she had strayed into a carefully constructed trap.

'Different!' exclaimed Amy. 'Dreamy. And yet you were definitely...upset. Yes, upset,' she added, her dramatic expression giving way to a worried look. 'What's happened, Flo? Or rather, did something happen between you and Signor Moneybags?'

'Will you please stop calling him that!' howled Flora.

'Just leave it, Amy,' said Brett sternly. 'It's none of our business.'

With a monumental effort Flora managed to snap out of her gloomy mood to dutifully play her part in the upcoming festivities. She put in a brief appearance at the New Year's party being held by one of Amy's doctor colleagues near the hospital where Amy and Brett had worked, and the following day she attended their small but exquisite wedding.

And somehow she didn't cry.

Even when clouds of confetti fluttered into the icy air in a blur of dried rose petals, not a single tear had leaked from her eye.

She'd even managed to keep a cheerful countenance when she returned to Heathrow Airport to wave the newly-weds off on their new life together, though once the massive airbus had taken to the skies, she had broken down completely—gulping convulsively into a paper hankie as she stood beside the vast, plate glass windows.

'You okay, love?'

Glancing up at the concerned face of a security guard, Flora had nodded. 'I'm fine!' she trilled, before noisily blowing her nose.

Except that she wasn't. She wasn't fine at all, not by anyone's measure, though it took a while before she was prepared to admit it.

At first she was too busy to think much about it,

welcoming Dante Antonelli into the office as the new CEO and making sure that everything ran smoothly. If anything, the former racing car driver was even better looking than Vito, but, unlike every other woman in the building, Flora barely noticed him.

She started keeping her head down, just like in the old days. She had vowed to seek out a different career path in the New Year and find something which suited her better, but suddenly she didn't have the energy. What had *happened* to her energy levels? Why had the lightest shower of rain started deterring her from cycling in to work, so that she would slouch onto the bus instead?

She knew why, no matter how much she tried to deny it.

She tried telling herself that even if she was pregnant—even if she *was*—then no way could she have known about it so early on.

But the truth was that she'd felt completely different from day one.

Would it be fanciful to conclude that she'd felt a tiny burst of something bright and fierce, just after Vito had made love to her—as if he had put brand new life in her? Maybe it would, but then she started feeling exceptionally tired in the afternoons and—controversially—she had gone right off lime marmalade. In fact, she couldn't face breakfast at all and it was usually her favourite meal of the day.

Eventually she was forced to face the incontrovertible evidence of two positive pregnancy tests done in quick succession in the cramped bathroom of her Ealing flat. Sitting back on her heels on the chilly lino, Flora stared in horror at the two blue lines which appeared on the tester. She thought back to the very last time they'd made love, all early morning sleepiness and fumbling fingers...had they failed to ensure the condom was properly in place before they started having sex?

Her heart was pounding and her mouth was dry.

She was going to have a baby.

The thought raced round and round inside her head, like a cyclist in a velodrome.

She was going to be a mother.

More than that, Vito Monticello was going to be a father.

A *father*.

It was worse than she could have thought possible. The Italian billionaire didn't want children. He'd *told* her that. Quite coldly and clearly.

Flora's fingers were shaking so much that she had to put the test down. If only she could have wound the clock back and behaved differently on that snowy night. She wouldn't have told Vito she fancied him—she would have kept that nugget of useless information to herself. She would have remained cool and aloof and ignored all the hot sexual chemistry which had been pulsing between them. And then he wouldn't have softly challenged her. Nor pushed her down on the rug and taken her panties off so that her thighs had parted eagerly, greedy for his thrust. He would have chivalrously slept on the sofa as he'd offered, while she would have been alone in that big brass bed. The worst thing that would have happened would have been having to endure a long and sleepless night while she thought longingly about the man downstairs.

And wouldn't that have been for the best? It might have kept her dreams manageable, which currently they were not. Because she couldn't deny a splinter of hope which had lodged itself in her foolish heart as she'd wondered whether Vito would change his mind about never wanting to see her again. Whether he would have second thoughts and ring her up, even if it was to carelessly enquire how she was doing. Or send a casual email, mentioning he was planning a trip to London and then maybe the conversation would have naturally worked its way to a suggested meet-up. At least she could have told him about the baby in a civilised way, if he invited her out to dinner. But he hadn't. There hadn't been a whisper from him and Flora had made herself accept the bitter truth. Not only did Vito Monticello not want any children, it seemed he didn't want a girlfriend either. Or at least, he didn't want her.

Had she really thought he would?

Hugging her arms around her chest, she rocked forwards and back, closing her eyes as troubled thoughts invaded her head. In a way she was glad Amy had left the country, because she didn't want anybody else's advice, no matter how well-meaning.

This had to be her decision and she knew without a shadow of a doubt that she was going to love this baby with all her heart. Because she knew about motherhood. She'd stepped in to raise her little sister when their mother had died and had loved doing it. Whatever fate threw at her, she would deal with. She would *manage*.

But the voice of her conscience wouldn't be silenced. Because…

What about Vito? Despite his aversion to fatherhood, surely he had a right to know he was going to be a dad. And if that were to be the case, then what was the correct protocol for imparting such a monumental piece of news? Should she pluck up courage and phone him, or maybe just pitch up at his Milanese headquarters and announce it without any kind of warning.

No.

That kind of dramatic confrontation might have been appropriate if they'd had been in some sort of relationship, but it had been nothing more than a one-night hookup. It wasn't ever supposed to be repeated and it wasn't supposed to have any repercussions. Imagining Vito's horror at discovering that she was carrying a Monticelli heir was all too easy and Flora wasn't feeling strong enough to stomach such a reaction. Nor to face the sniggers of the workers in his Italian office with whom she'd spoken many times.

It turned out that procrastination was easier than confrontation. So she put off doing anything.

February came and went, and soon the first buds of spring appeared in some of the window boxes along her road. She should have been cheered by the sight of all those miniature yellow daffodils pushing through the wet brown soil but for once the advent of spring was refusing to inspire her.

And then the sickness started. Without any kind of warning she'd be forced to rush to the loo at work and, more than once, she caught Dante Antonelli regarding her curiously when she returned to the office, pale-faced and dry-mouthed and trying very hard not to tremble.

'You are not well,' he observed one morning, his dark eyes narrowing.

'I think I must have some sort of bug!'

'Again?'

Was she imagining the thoughtful tone of his reply? Was he thinking she was useless as a secretary and about to ring HR to ask how best she could be replaced and if that were the case, what would she *do*? If people found out she was pregnant they'd want to know who the father was and unless she was planning on trying to carry off a virgin birth, imagine their shock if they discovered it was the boss!

And although the sickness receded as swiftly as it had arrived, she knew she couldn't carry on like this, pretending nothing was the matter. She would ring Vito at the weekend—when he wasn't busy and she wasn't distracted—and she would tell him her news *very calmly*. What he did with that piece of information was up to him, but she would let him know that she was prepared to be reasonable.

Flora awoke on Saturday morning to the heavy pound of rain. Wind was whistling through the gap in the window frame and, after shivering in the shower, she bundled on her thickest sweater and a pair of Amy's jeans which were slightly too short for her, before making some weak tea. Carrying her mug into the sitting room, she sat down on the battered sofa and started rehearsing the words she would say when she finally plucked up enough courage to dial the international number, when a loud ring on the doorbell startled her out of her reverie.

Was it her hipster neighbour Joe from upstairs? she wondered. Offering her one of his homemade brownies, or asking if she had any camomile teabags? Amy had been certain the geeky designer fancied her, but Flora hadn't been convinced. Anyway, the most eligible man on the planet could have asked her out and she would have just looked at him blankly, because who in the world could have compared to Vito Monticello?

She opened the door by a crack, her polite smile dying when she saw who was standing there and for a moment Flora thought she must have magicked him up from her frenzied thoughts.

But this man wasn't a figment of anyone's imagination.

This man was real.

Very, very real.

And angry.

Not a raging kind of anger, but a quiet and infinitely more deadly kind, which simmered at the back of his ice-blue eyes.

Why was he angry? she speculated with a sudden sinking feeling of apprehension.

'Vito!' she said.

'You look surprised, Flora,' he observed, his silken tone underpinned with something which sounded like...

Danger?

Tiny droplets of rain glinted like jewels in his ebony hair and his dark and golden beauty was so intense that it quite simply took her breath away, just as it had done the first time she'd seen him. And oh, how she wanted him. Flora swallowed. It was as instant and as complete as that. She felt a part of him. Was that because she was carrying his baby inside her?

Sucking in a deep breath, she sought to compose herself. 'Of course I'm surprised! It's a long way from Milan! Why...why didn't you warn me you were coming?'

'I think,' he said, and his voice sounded as if it had been coated in some dark and corrosive liquid, 'that if there are any questions to be asked, then I should be the one seeking answers. Don't you?'

A shiver of apprehension whispered down Flora's spine. 'Not if—'

'Is everything okay, Flo?' came a concerned voice, and Flora looked over the shoulder of the Italian billionaire, up to see Joe coming down the communal stairs, his brow creased with concern.

She saw Vito shoot the pony-tailed designer a look of dislike.

'I'm fine, Joe. Thanks for asking.' But she didn't introduce the two men, just opened the door a little wider and sent a pointed look at her ex-boss. 'I suppose you'd better come in.'

'At last!' he snarled sarcastically.

Steeling himself against what he might find, Vito followed Flora into her ground-floor apartment, his heart sinking as he looked around. It was worse than he'd imagined. But then, he'd never been anywhere like this before. A tiny sitting room crammed with mismatched furniture which overlooked a busy street. A small table was pushed against a wall, a cheap television sat on a shelf and next to it, a bookcase sagged from the weight of all the books. And it was cold. Bitterly cold.

Turning to Flora, he looked at her properly for the first time, his gaze scanning over her, unable to prevent the arrow of shock which shot through him. Her face was as white as marble and there were shadows beneath her green-gold eyes. Her cheekbones were hollow and pinched and she looked as if she might have lost weight, though it was difficult to tell beneath that jumper. He felt the twist of something inexplicable in his heart but hot on the heels of guilt, came rage.

What was she trying to hide?

You know damned well what she's trying to hide.

Part of him wanted to test her by prevaricating. To see how long it would take for her to admit the truth. But what was the point of trying to see if she would attempt to pull the wool over his eyes and fool him, just so he could gain some kind of moral advantage? This was way too serious. 'Do you have something you want to tell me?' he questioned coolly.

He saw her swallow, saw the sudden spring of tears to her eyes and he had to fight the urge to pull her into his arms. To comfort her, or to kiss her, he wasn't quite sure. But kissing her would be sending out mixed messages and comforting her would confuse the hell out of *him*. Don't fail her by letting her think you're the kind of man you can never be, he told himself fiercely. Don't start acting in a way you'll be unable to sustain.

'So,' he said, while still she continued to look at him, her extraordinary eyes hooded and wary, her lips trembling as she drove her teeth into them. As if she were reluctant to say the words which would change everything.

'I'm having a baby,' she said at last.

CHAPTER EIGHT

VITO STARED INTO Flora's eyes and even though deep down he had been expecting those words, her confirmation of her condition pained him all the same. 'You think I don't know that?' he snapped.

Her eyes grew startled. 'How?' she whispered. 'How can you possibly know I'm pregnant?'

'I rang Dante.'

'But... I don't understand. Dante is my new boss, what does he have to do with anything?'

The emotion of this meeting had definitely impacted on her, because she was blinking at him, her feathery lashes suddenly sparkling with tears, and with a pang Vito remembered the last time he'd seen her cry. When he'd brought her pleasure so sweet that she had wept— and yet how far away such pleasure seemed right now.

'How can he know?' she whispered, her lashes batting up and down as she attempted to clear her vision. 'Nobody does.'

'Wipe your eyes,' he commanded roughly, pulling a pristine handkerchief from his jacket and pressing it into her hand, flinching from the touch of her soft flesh as he recalled the recent nightmare escalation of events.

He had convinced himself it was nothing but mild curiosity which had compelled him to ring Verdenergia's new CEO to enquire how Flora was getting along, though deep down he hadn't been able to stop thinking about her. He'd been dreaming about her every night, waking up rock-hard and frustrated and covered in sweat. Yet it wasn't just sexual recall which had filled him with restlessness, but some insane yearning for the easy familiarity he had enjoyed with her, much to his surprise and irritation. He'd told himself that his mild obsession was merely a result of not having had time to grow tired of her. Latterly, he had convinced himself that news of her mundane comings and goings in the office would be enough to kill his desire for her, which surely would have been the most appropriate outcome all round.

And then there had been the shock of Dante's words and his own horrified comprehension as their significance had sunk in.

He ran his thumb along the edge of his jaw, recognising with alarm that he had forgotten to shave. Such lack of attention to his usually immaculate appearance was unheard of, for Vito was fastidious about maintaining a cool carapace to present to the world. Had that been the reason his pilot had regarded him so oddly this morning, or had it been his sudden demand to fly to England as quickly as possible?

Throughout the flight he had been unable to process his thoughts and it wasn't until his jet touched down that he became filled with one certainty—that he must be true to himself. For a man incapable of giving or receiving love, what choice did he have than to spare the feelings of others? Why inflict his emotional indifference on a wife or a child? Which was why he wasn't going to offer Flora Greening anything he couldn't deliver and in the long run, he would be doing her a favour. He had come here today to coolly inform her that he would have his lawyers draw up a watertight agreement, offering financial support for her and the child, but nothing else.

Nothing.

He stared into her green-gold eyes and suddenly he had to work very hard to remain cold and indifferent. 'Dante wondered why you kept rushing from the office to be sick,' he bit out. 'He said you reminded him of one of his sisters when she was pregnant. And that he had no idea you were married—'

'*Married?*' she cut in. 'What's that got to do with anything?'

'For someone who is the same age as me, he has some very old-fashioned ideas.' His gaze scanned her belly again, as if by looking hard enough he would be able to see through the thick wool of her sweater. 'How far gone are you, Flora?'

His words seemed to trigger something, because suddenly the linger of tears had been replaced by sparks of angry gold flashing from her green eyes. 'Let's skip the injured innocent act shall we, Vito? You know exactly how far gone I am! We had sex two days before Christmas which makes me three months pregnant. My baby is due in the middle of September.'

'*Your* baby?'

She stared at him in sudden confusion. 'I thought you'd be pleased at the let-out clause. You made your feelings on fatherhood clear,' she said, but he heard the faint tremble in her voice. 'You never want to get married, remember? You never want a family of your own.'

'And both those things are true.' He saw her flinch. 'Is that why you didn't tell me?'

'I *was* planning to tell you!'

'When?' he grated. 'When you were wheeling the infant in a stroller for a walk around *Ealing*? Or were you planning on waiting until graduation?'

'I was actually planning to ring you up today.'

'Wow, what an amazing coincidence,' he said sarcastically.

'Life is full of coincidences, Vito—haven't you learnt that by now?' She sucked in a shuddering breath. 'Listen, there's no point in you being angry, or me reacting to your anger, because it isn't helpful to anyone. It is what it is. I'm not planning on asking you for anything and I certainly don't expect you to slide a gold band on my finger.'

'Well, that's good since I'm right out of gold bands,' he drawled and, as her eyelids shuttered down to hide her hurt expression, he wondered if his words had been unnecessarily cruel. But it was the truth, wasn't it? Wasn't it better she accepted his heartlessness from the get-go, in case she started concocting some kind of fantasy happy-ever-after? 'But that doesn't mean that I am unwilling to help in other ways,' he conceded. 'Which is why I am here today.'

'You should have saved yourself the trip. I don't need your help!'

'Are you quite sure about that?' With a sweeping gesture, he indicated the cramped dimensions of the tiny room—the battered sofa and faded curtains which fluttered in the chill that was seeping in through the window. 'You think this is a good place to bring up a baby?'

Flora willed herself not to get emotional as Vito continued to talk so coldly and dispassionately about the tiny life she carried, but a terrible sadness had started welling up inside her, along with a familiar wave of nausea—the first she'd had in almost a fortnight. 'I have to go!' she gulped, stumbling from the room towards the bathroom, glad to have an excuse to escape the scrutiny of that icy stare.

Turning on the taps full blast, she hoped the rush of water would disguise the sound of her retching and once the sickness had passed, she brushed her teeth rather violently, raked a brush through her hair and shuddered at the image reflected back at her in the tiny mirror above the sink. She looked awful. Drained and drawn and the antithesis of how a glowing pregnant woman was supposed to look. It was the last way she would have wished to present herself to him, until she reminded herself that what she looked like was irrelevant.

Reluctantly, she made her way back towards the sitting room, registering the incongruous spectacle of Vito Monticelli dominating her tiny flat. With his powerful body silhouetted against the rain-splashed window, it was hard to look anywhere other than at him. She noticed he had removed his overcoat and was wearing jaded jeans and a soft sweater a shade darker than his eyes. She realised she'd never seen him dressed so casually before and there was something dangerously accessible about this laid-back version of the Italian billionaire. Pared down, his sex appeal was just as potent and Flora was surprised by the sudden curl of longing inside her. Be careful, she thought suddenly. Be very, very careful.

His icy-blue gaze pierced through her. 'You have been sick?' he demanded.

'Only a bit. It's the first time in a couple of weeks. Don't worry. It's perfectly normal.'

'No. *No lo so!* None of this is *normal*!' he contradicted, drawing in an impatient breath before pointing to one of the two modest armchairs. 'You are pale, Flora—for god's sake sit down.'

Flora was about to protest that he couldn't start coming in here throwing his weight around, but one look at the tension which was making his features tighten made her accept she had to cut him some slack. The news must have come as a terrible shock to him too, she acknowledged, putting aside her own wounded pride. And the sickness *had* left her feeling weak.

'Look, I'm sorry I didn't tell you before,' she said awkwardly, slumping into the nearby chair and sinking back into the cushions with a feeling of relief. 'But I was shocked too. I couldn't get my head around it and I didn't know how you were going to take it.' She still didn't know. 'Anyway, I've been managing okay.'

'You think so? You don't look as if you're managing to me, not by any stretch of the imagination,' he accused. 'You've lost weight, you look exhausted and it's freezing in here.'

'It's not f-freezing,' she argued, though annoyingly her teeth had started to chatter. Maybe that was word association. 'Okay, it's a bit cold, I agree. But this is England, not Italy—in case you hadn't noticed.'

His click of impatience made clear that now was not the time for levity. 'This place is not suitable for you to have a child.'

She looked at him in exasperation. 'How do you think most women manage, Vito? They have babies in ordinary places just like this!'

'I think your situation is a little different from *most women*.'

'Why?' she demanded. 'Because I'm pregnant by a man who never wanted to see me again and is a long-time opponent of family life? Or because you happen to be obscenely rich?'

'Flora, Flora, Flora,' he intoned placatingly. 'Please. Stop. I don't think that kind of attitude is helping.'

'Stop speaking the truth, you mean? Don't you *dare* patronise me, Vito Monticelli!'

She clenched her hands and for a moment it looked as if she might be about to launch herself out of the chair and punch her fists against his chest. And wasn't there a part of Vito which wished she would, so that he could cradle her petite body to his as he had been longing to do for weeks? So he could feel all that soft, curving warmth beneath his questing fingers and claim her trembling lips with his own—blotting out this unwanted reality she had presented to him, with the sweet oblivion of sex.

'Let's cut to the chase,' he said thickly, angry with the erotic distraction of his thoughts. 'What do you envisage happening next?'

She looked startled. 'Well, I guess I'll just carry on until I'm too big to work. And then I'll take maternity leave and then I'll... I'll...'

Deliberately, Vito allowed the silence to grow as her words tailed off. She really hadn't thought this through, he realised, with a flicker of impatience. 'That isn't going to work, I'm afraid,' he said, at last. 'Your current condition isn't compatible with being secretary to the CEO.'

'Ah, so *that's* where this is headed, is it?' She tilted her chin with proud defiance. 'Well, good luck with trying to sack me! There are laws against such things, you know.'

For a moment he almost laughed, her suggestion was so outrageous. 'I am a twenty-first-century businessman, Flora,' he offered dryly. 'Do you really think I'm capable of trying to enforce such outdated ideas?'

'How should I know what you're capable of when you barge in here as if you own the place?' she said, only now her voice had started wavering. 'I don't really know you at all.'

'In that case, there are a great many things we need to address.'

'Have your office type me out a list and I'll get round to reading it sometime!'

More used to a red carpet being rolled out for him than dealing with a stubborn woman so obviously in thrall to her raging hormones, Vito refused to rise to a flippancy which was, annoyingly, more than a little appealing. Because not only was it a mistake to allow her feistiness to weave its strangely sensual spell—couldn't he detect a deep fatigue which was underpinning her brittle air of defiance?

He remembered what she'd told him about her own family. She had never known her father, her mother was dead and her sister was in Australia. She might have friends, but what good were friends when the bills needed paying and the air was chilled? She was completely on her own. *What choice did he have but to help her?* 'You need to pack a bag.'

She looked at him blankly. 'A bag?'

'Just bring the basics with you,' he continued coolly, pulling his cell phone from his pocket. 'Everything else you need can easily be acquired later.'

'You're not making yourself clear,' she said.

'I cannot leave you here on your own.'

'I've lived here for years,' she told him, from between gritted teeth.

'But you weren't pregnant then,' he reminded her acidly. 'Does Amy know about your condition?'

At this she froze, a look of alarm shadowing her face. 'No! I didn't want to worry her and...'

'And?' he queried, thinking that she might do better if she stopped thinking about Amy all the time and started thinking about herself.

'I thought you should be... I wanted you to be the first. To know,' she concluded unsteadily.

This unexpected streak of consideration was oddly affecting and for a moment Vito was silent as a wave of compassion swept over him. 'So who is going to look after you?' he demanded. 'Unless you are depending on the guy with the ponytail?'

'I'm sure Joe would be happy to help with the shopping.'

'Oh, I'm sure he would,' he said, his voice silky soft.

'Are you jealous of Joe, Vito?'

'Why?' He stared her down. 'Should I be?'

'No. He's just a friend.' He saw her cheeks grow pink. 'Though that's not really the point.'

He gave an impatient wave of his hand. 'My mind is made up, Flora. You will have to return to Italy with me.'

A disbelieving pause spread out.

'*Really?*' she breathed. 'I'm not sure I understand. Wh-what...what's in it for you?'

Vito watched as a series of reactions flickered over her features. He saw shock, and surprise, and hope. Yes. There was definitely hope. And not only was hope a waste of time—it was one of the most difficult things to kill off. He'd seen it on the faces of women before. Too many to count. Ruthlessly he sought to make his intentions crystal-clear. 'This is simply a temporary measure. I can't promise you anything.'

'I'm not asking you to *promise* me anything!' she flared furiously. 'I'm not a small child waiting for Christmas!'

'I have a home in Milan which is easily big enough to accommodate you for a month or two until the sickness has passed,' he continued carefully.

'What about my job?'

'Do not concern yourself about that. I will arrange to have someone replace you while you're away.'

Was it the suggestion that she was so easily replaceable which caused all the emotion to drain from her face, so that it resembled nothing more than a blank canvas?

'Thank you, Vito,' she said quietly, the shining tumble of her curls moving as she nodded. 'It's a very... generous...offer. But it's a bad idea.'

His eyes narrowed. 'Because?'

'I don't have to tell you every thought that's going around in my head,' she defended vigorously. 'I just don't want to go to Milan and you can't make me.'

'You think so?' he said softly.

'Try me!' she challenged.

So he did. Sitting down in the chair opposite her Vito began to speak, softly at first—while for much of the time, she glared at him. But his determination did not waver. No matter how much Flora railed against his resolve, he was ready for her. This time he would do the right thing. He would be able to live with the knowledge that he had done what was best for her, no matter what the eventual outcome might be. So he cajoled and he coaxed—shamelessly listing the many advantages of being under his protection—which easily overshadowed all her reasons for staying. Every objection she raised he had an answer for, until eventually she nodded, holding up the palms of her hands and giving a heavy sigh of mock surrender.

'Okay, Vito,' she said 'You win. I'll come to Milan. For a short while, at least.'

But the defiant glint in her green-gold eyes remained and Vito wondered if that was what stopped him from reminding her that he *always* won.

CHAPTER NINE

SUDDENLY FLORA FOUND herself channelling Alice in Wonderland.

The girl from Ealing was on her way to Milan, mostly due to the persistence of the Italian billionaire.

Not that she had allowed Vito Monticello to have everything his own way. She had firmly put the brakes on the tycoon's speedy agenda. She told him that no way would she accompany him to Italy the moment he snapped his commanding fingers, insisting on a few days' grace to make her small flat pristine for the duration of her absence.

'Why?' he had demanded impatiently. 'Let me have an agency do that for you.'

'No. I want to do it myself,' she had objected stubbornly. But it wasn't simply because she needed time to stop and gather her breath and try to get her head around what was happening. Wasn't the truth that it gave her a kick to defy him? She enjoyed seeing the look of surprise in his eyes, as if he were used to women doing exactly what he wanted.

She gave a set of keys to Joe, who promised to water her plants and keep everything ticking over until she knew what her plans were. Because Flora knew she needed to cling onto her independence. She needed a base to come back to. A place to run to.

Yet things had changed, and she had to change with them.

No longer a stranger to private aviation, Vito's jet wasn't quite so intimidating this time around and the enormous limousine waiting for them at the Milanese airfield didn't faze her one bit. But as the uniformed driver opened the rear door and she slid inside, Flora knew she hadn't imagined his curious glance. Was he thinking that this rather ordinary Englishwoman was very different from his boss's usual partners?

But she wasn't Vito's partner, was she? More like his lodger. And a temporary one at that, he had made that abundantly clear. As they drove through the busy streets of the city, she snuck a glance at him, all dark and sexy and delicious, jabbering away on his phone in Italian as the car purred past the monuments and as always, her stomach melted. He had turned up at her flat this morning, wearing a charcoal suit which was quite literally traffic-stopping—judging by the two women on the school run whose cars almost collided because they were so busy gawping at him.

She mustn't get used to living like this or taking these kinds of conveniences for granted, she told herself. The fancy planes and cars were nothing but the transitory benefits of carrying a wealthy man's child and Vito certainly wasn't offering anything other than a very brief refuge.

Not marriage, or permanence or any suggestion that he intended to be part of their baby's life.

And certainly nothing which would come even close to love.

So stop thinking about it, she warned herself fiercely—or rather, stop thinking about him in the romantic sense. Concentrate on giving all your love to this little being inside you. This innocent child who didn't asked to be conceived. The baby he hasn't even mentioned since he'd got his way over bringing her here.

Her sister had expressed grave doubts when Flora had finally made her bombshell pregnancy disclosure. Originally cautioning her against putting herself in Vito's territory, Amy had changed her mind when her sister had confessed to being sick.

'Well, since there's nobody else around to do it, you'd better tell Vito Monticello to take good care of you,' she had announced grimly. 'Or he'll have me to deal with!'

Flora would like to have been a fly on the wall to see *that* happen. She had bitten back the accusation which was hovering on her lips—that her sister had in some way helped facilitate the inappropriate liaison with her boss with her gift of sexy undies. And she hadn't even told Amy the whole story—that a strange sense of contentment had crept over her from the moment Vito had stormed back into her life. Because wasn't there something supremely comforting about having the powerful tycoon take over and look after her? For the first time ever she felt as if she could let someone else do the worrying and that felt like a pretty big deal.

And wasn't that a crazy thing to be thinking?

'We're here,' Vito announced, sliding his phone back inside his pocket as the car entered an impressive square with an unusual bell-like sculpture at its centre. A careless wave of his hand indicated an impressive-looking modern building towering above them. 'This is the Piazza San Babila and my home is right here.'

'Home' it seemed, was a penthouse apartment which occupied three whole floors.

'*Three* floors?' Flora verified incredulously.

He nodded.

'All for you?'

'All for me,' he agreed, with the ghost of a smile. 'I like my personal space.'

'Yet you live in a city?'

'Oh, believe me.' His eyes glittered. 'It's easy to be anonymous in a city.'

'Okay, I get it, Vito. I'll try not to impinge on your personal space *too* much.'

'Good.'

She insisted on him giving her 'the tour' because she wanted to see it through his eyes as well as to get her bearings and, although he seemed somewhat taken aback by her request, he complied, taking her through room after glamorous room. But Flora couldn't help thinking that Vito's apartment looked more like pictures from a glossy magazine, than a place where real people lived. The ceilings were high and the decor achingly modern. Spectacular chandeliers glittered their light onto large velvet sofas and sumptuous drapes framed the cityscape, but the atmosphere felt almost *antiseptic*. As if he'd given a very expensive interior designer carte blanche to do as they pleased. Only his study provided a glimpse of the man behind the shiny patina of success, although initially he tried to steer her past it.

'You're saying it's out of bounds?' she dared to tease.

'No, I'm not saying that at all,' he growled reluctantly, throwing open the door for her to step inside.

Flora prowled around the room with interest, studying the various industry awards which littered his desk. The statuette which proclaimed him a clean-energy titan. A framed front cover of *Time* magazine on the wall, with his coldly beautiful face regarding the camera with more than a little mocking defiance. Behind his desk was a photo of a much younger Vito in the University of Bologna football team and a framed MBA from Harvard.

'I didn't know you'd been to America,' she observed.

'That's where I started my tech business.' His ice-blue eyes were hooded and he nodded as he registered her surprise. 'I was successful in my own right, long before my father died. I bought this place with my own money,' he added brusquely, as if this mattered.

'Right,' said Flora, absorbing this piece of information as she scanned the contents of his bookshelves and there, pushed into the background and almost swallowed up by the volume of books surrounding them, were some photos.

Three photos, to be precise. Flora bent down to peer at the first. A man of around seventy—his lined and handsome face so like Vito's own. Next to it was a portrait of a beautiful woman in her prime—her shoulders bare, with just the hint of white fur beneath and, wrapped around her slender neck, was a collar of sparkling aquamarines which matched her ice-blue eyes exactly.

'Your mum and dad?' Flora verified.

'*Si*,' he agreed brusquely. 'Come, Flora. That's enough. I have a busy schedule.'

'In a minute.' Refusing to be rushed, she bent to study the final photo of a man younger than Vito but just as beautiful, though his eyes were dark, not blue. Yet this wasn't a happy snap, she thought suddenly. His face was bleak and unsmiling, his hair untidily long and there was something awfully *empty* about his eyes. 'Is this your brother?'

'*Si.*'

She'd noticed before that he automatically lapsed into Italian when he was tense and although he used this particular word forbiddingly, Flora took no notice—and not just because she was curious to know more about her baby's ancestors. It was because he'd told her his brother was dead and she knew the worst thing you could do was to pretend that a person had never existed. Hadn't that been what had happened when Mum had died? People had literally crossed over to the other side of the road because they hadn't known what to say to her or Amy. And even though it was often painful to recall the person you'd lost—that didn't mean you shouldn't do it.

'You don't look very alike,' she offered truthfully.

'We weren't alike. Not in any way.' His voice was abrasive as he pulled open the study door and now there was no mistaking his determination to get her out of there. 'Come on now, Flora. I have a call to the States I need to make before dinner and I can't waste any more time talking to you.'

'Well, since you ask so nicely,' she said sarcastically as she followed him into one of the vast reception rooms and he rang a bell to summon his staff.

A housekeeper called Marisa and a smiley cook called Mafalda trooped in, accompanied by two of Mafalda's daughters, who came in on a daily basis to keep the enormous place clean. They all shook Flora's hand and looked her up and down with friendly interest.

'They all speak excellent English,' Vito informed her, once the small deputation had filed out. 'So you shouldn't have any problem making yourself understood.'

'So the only communication problem I'm going to have is with you, is it, Vito?'

'What are you talking about?'

She sighed. 'Well, you and I speak the same language but that didn't stop you riding roughshod over my desire to stay in England, did it?' Or from effectively refusing to talk about his family.

'Please don't make me out to be the big, bad wolf just because it suits your narrative, Flora,' he retorted, his eyes glittering. 'If you really hadn't wanted to come, then you wouldn't be here. It isn't as if I kidnapped you and transported you here rolled up in a carpet, is it?'

'That's not funny.'

'Yet you're laughing,' he observed dryly.

'I am *not* laughing.' She clamped her lips together, feeling the unwanted rise of her pulse in response to his soft statement. Because something in the way he was looking at her was making her blood fizz. The smoulder of his eyes had ignited a slow fire, which was causing a sweet ache to unfurl low in her belly. It was the sweetly potent lick of desire, she acknowledged weakly and wondered if he was feeling it too. Did he want to pick up where they'd left off? Yes, *please*, she found herself thinking.

'Let me show you to your room,' he said suddenly.

His cool assertion shattered her erotic thoughts and Flora was angry with herself. How could she have allowed herself to be that vulnerable when she had *known*—or rather, guessed—they wouldn't be sharing a bedroom? He hadn't touched her since he'd blazed into her London life and turned it upside down, had he? His stated intention to bring her here had sounded more like a powerful man negotiating a business deal. It hadn't been tinged with any affection, or desire, and he had gone out of his way to emphasise the transitory place she held in his life. He had regarded her with nothing but caution since he'd found out about the pregnancy—as if she was a ticking time bomb which could go off at any second.

She'd even tried convincing herself she would be outraged if he suggested having sex again. But deep down she knew that was a big, fat lie and there had been a moment back then when she'd been overcome with it. Chemistry, or lust—or whatever you chose to call it. The inconvenient attraction which had got them into this crazy situation in the first place. In truth, she'd wanted him to pull her into his arms and ravish the hell out of her, while he had been as cool as a cucumber.

Somehow, she maintained her rictus of a smile. 'Sure. Let's go.'

Her room overlooked the square. A bed as big as a football pitch, floaty drapes which hung beside the floor-to-ceiling windows and vibrant artwork on the walls. Flora walked over to the window and stared down at the piazza. It was late afternoon and people were crowding into the fashionable space—strolling and shopping. Some were drinking early cocktails in select little bars and a couple of children were eating gelato. Down there the normal and everyday was carrying on as usual—while up here, she found herself in the most extraordinary situation. And suddenly she started longing for her old life with a pang which was almost physical. She might have been poor and ordinary, but at least back in England she felt as if she fitted in.

She turned to see Vito watching her, his eyes narrowed.

'You don't like it?'

'It's wonderful,' she said automatically.

He frowned, as if her lack of enthusiasm was not what he had been expecting. 'I'll have some tea sent up, and then you can get some rest before dinner.'

'I'm not an invalid, Vito.'

'No, you're not,' he agreed, his gaze skating over her with critical assessment. 'But you look tired and it's been a long day.'

And in a way his consideration was the worst of all possible worlds because it created the illusion that he cared and Flora had to keep reminding herself that he didn't. She was a burden. She'd brought something into his life which he resented. If only she'd had the courage to tell him to stop behaving so solicitously towards her, but he was already closing the door behind him and in truth, she *was* tired. Really tired. She drank the camomile tea which Mafalda brought her and the older woman's kindness as she began to fuss around with the pillows made Flora feel stupidly emotional and she grew impatient with herself. Why choose *now* of all times, to feel sentimental about not having a mum when she'd managed so well for all these years without one?

At least the fancy bathroom provided a welcome diversion, with its sparkling mirrors and rows of fancy toiletries—though the images reflected back seemed to reinforce her outsider status. Her clothes weren't *too* bad. She was still able to fit into Amy's stuff—just about. But her hair could do with a wash and her comfy trainers had seen better days. Tipping in a generous amount of scented oil, she ran a deep bath, stripping off her clothes, before gingerly lowering herself into the fragrant bubbles.

It was bliss—and as different from the lukewarm trickle in the bathroom of her Ealing flat as it was possible to imagine. She lay there for longer than she'd intended, staring down at the nipples which were just peeping through the white foam, thinking how much darker they were than before. And despite her slew of concerns, she found herself studying her rapidly changing body with a degree of interest, until she began to yawn and knew she really needed to wash the oil from her hair and get out.

She wrapped herself in a fluffy white bathrobe and

wondered if she ought to get dressed but the bed was as soft as a marshmallow and too inviting to resist. She thought of getting underneath the duvet but somehow she couldn't seem to summon up the energy. So she snuggled down and fell asleep—though at one point she could have sworn she felt something soft and warm drifting down on top of her, which made her murmur her appreciation. And when she opened her eyes, the sky had grown dusky and she was lying beneath a cashmere throw and there was Vito on the other side of the room, staring out of the tall windows, his body as motionless as a dark and beautiful statue.

She blinked, her hungry gaze drinking him in, wondering if she was still dreaming. His immaculate suit had been replaced by black jeans and sweater—and the fact that he had changed possessed a strange kind of intimacy all of its own. They might not be sharing a bed but they were certainly sharing an apartment and Flora had never lived with a man before. Silhouetted against the pricking lights of the darkening city, his body was the epitome of masculine power and Flora found herself responding to it on a purely instinctual level. It felt so *right* for him to be in her bedroom. So ridiculously right and, just for that split-second—it was all too easy to pretend they were still lovers.

'What time is it?' she enquired sleepily.

Vito turned away from the window, his throat growing dry as he surveyed the woman on the bed. 'Nearly dinner time,' he answered thickly. 'I came to wake you.' But she had looked so damned angelic that he hadn't wanted to disturb her. He hadn't dared reach down to shake one slender shoulder, for fear that his fingers might stray beneath her robe, to caress the warm, swollen curve of her breast...

Brushing her fingers back through tousled curls, she sat up and yawned. 'How long have I been asleep?'

'Nearly two hours. You called out at one point—I think you were having a bad dream. I came in and you were shivering, so I covered you up.'

She looked down at the cashmere blanket and then smiled up at him. 'Thanks.'

He wanted to tell her not to look at him like that, because it was making him want things he had cautioned himself against. To kiss her and stroke her. To make her wet and quivering until she was angling those delicious hips with urgent invitation as she waited for his thrust.

She shouldn't have looked quite so alluring, he thought resentfully. Not with her bare face still flushed with sleep and her hair sticking up at odd angles. But alluring she undoubtedly was and all he wanted was to lose himself in her tight heat. But he was supposed to be protecting her and, having convinced himself that behaving like a benign guardian was in her best interests, he knew that sex would be a mistake. Of course it would. It would blur the boundaries. It would create the illusion of togetherness and make her start to hope. She would become besotted with him—as women invariably did. He would end up hurting her and no way did he want to hurt her.

'Dinner will be in half an hour,' he said, clicking on the overhead light in the hope that additional illumination might shatter some of the sensual atmosphere. 'I'll see you downstairs.'

'No. Don't go yet, Vito. There are a couple of things I need to ask you first.'

'Like what?' he queried coolly.

'What you've told people about me, and why I'm here.' She shrugged as he continued to stare at her uncomprehendingly. 'Your friends, for example—and your staff.'

He raked impatient fingers through his hair. 'I have told them nothing.'

'What?' She stared very hard at him. 'Nothing at all?'

'No.' Vito knew that her presence would provoke debate in the more fevered salons of the fashionable city, who surveyed the comings and goings of one of Italy's most eligible bachelors with jealous scrutiny. A pregnant stranger staying at the home of Vito Monticello was always going to whet the appetite of any gossip. But he was powerful and resilient enough not to care what people said about him, because the worst had already happened in his life and nothing else could ever feel that bad again. 'We don't have to tell them anything,' he concluded roughly.

She was staring at him as if he'd just grown a second head. 'Are you crazy?'

'What's the problem?'

'The problem is that I'm *pregnant* and yes, I can see that word is making you flinch, Vito, even though you're trying to hide it—so just imagine the reaction of other people. Very soon I'm going to start to show. And then what?'

'You tell me,' he said, feeling completely out of his depth. And it wasn't a nice feeling.

'At first they'll just think I'm one of your usual live-in girlfriends—'

'But I've never had a live-in girlfriend,' he growled.

'Oh. Right. Well, that's irrelevant.' She looked startled and then noisily cleared her throat, which he supposed was intended to divert attention from her undeniable smile. 'So how are you going to explain it to people when they see me expanding?'

'Don't your own British royal family talk about never complaining and never explaining?' he demanded. 'Why should I say anything?'

'That is such a naive question—I can't actually believe you asked it! Because otherwise they'll speculate. That's what people do. If that's what you want, then fine. But if we're going to pretend this is not your baby, then we'll need to get our story straight.'

Vito stared at her, unable to hide his sudden dismay. It hadn't occurred to him to explain away Flora's presence in his life by fabricating a story and his body tensed with outraged objection. He was *not* going to lie about this child's paternity. For hadn't he learnt the folly of lying, in the most bitter way of all? And hadn't she put all that to the forefront of his mind earlier, with her innocent observations about his brother?

'Are you happy for me to introduce you as the mother of my child?' he demanded.

'I don't know if "happy" is the right word. If you do that, then people will assume you're planning to be a hands-on father.' She took a deep breath, her green-gold eyes huge. 'And you don't want that, do you, Vito?'

There was a pause during which he could hear the beep of a car horn in the distance. 'No,' he said abruptly, staring out of the window again as he glanced down at the Piazza San Babila. His gaze was unfocused and all he could see was a blur, but it gave him a chance to gather his thoughts and remove himself from her line of vision.

He had been right when he'd told her that he preferred his own company, although that didn't stop people from constantly seeking him out in the city he had adopted in preference to his native Rome. The organisers of the glitziest gallery openings, high-profile parties and first nights waited with bated breath to see if Vito Monticello would grace their event with his presence, but he refused far more invitations than those he accepted. He was easily bored and it was always the same conversations. The same faces.

But Flora's face was different. *She* was different, in ways too many to count. Fresh and unsophisticated. Relatively naive and, always, breathtakingly honest. Wouldn't it be like throwing a hunk of glistening meat to a pack of wolves if he told people she was having his baby, while offering her nothing tangible in the way of security? Didn't he owe her that much, at least?

He turned back to survey her, his throat growing tight. 'We could say we're engaged.'

'I thought you didn't want to get married.'

He gave a short laugh. 'I most certainly don't. I'm not talking about a real engagement, but an illusory one. It will provide you with security and alleviate the sense of responsibility I feel towards you.'

'Gosh. How grim that sounds.' She pulled a face. 'Like I'm some intolerable burden!'

'Melodrama isn't particularly helpful in the circumstances, Flora,' he drawled. 'I'm trying to be pragmatic. Being my fiancée will give you a certain…*status* in Milanese society—although it will inevitably subject you to a degree of scrutiny. Possibly envy,' he concluded thoughtfully.

'Oh, dear. Will I have to withstand a hail of missiles from heartbroken females every time I set foot outside the door?'

'I don't think things will descend to quite that level,' he murmured, with the glimmer of a smile. 'Do you think you can bear to do it?' There was a pause. 'Do you *want* to do it?'

'That depends. Will we have to pretend to be in love?'

'I don't think I'm that good an actor,' he offered dryly.

'Ouch. You really don't pull your punches, do you, Vito?'

'Do you want me to lie to you?'

Well, yes. Flora pulled a face. Sometimes, she did. Sometimes she wanted to hear things he was never going to say. 'I suppose not.'

'So, we have a solution. Be my fiancée. At least for show, in public. Just while you're here. It isn't going to be for long, is it?' he added softly.

Flora bit her lip. He obviously couldn't wait to see the back of her!

'Not only will you miss out on being a social pariah,'

he continued. 'But you'll get a big diamond ring to wear, which should provide a little in the way of compensation.' His mouth flattened into a grimace of a smile. 'Judging by how much women seem to value diamonds.'

Flora stared at him, hating the cynical timbre of his voice. Did he really think the entire female sex was that shallow—or that he needed to placate her with expensive toys? It seemed a waste of time to tell him she thought diamonds were cold and unimaginative. They certainly weren't forever. Not in this case.

But his words contained a strange kind of sense, despite the impersonal way he had delivered them. An engagement would guarantee her respectability, even if it wasn't real. Because what was the alternative? People looking at her pityingly, or angrily—outraged that this little nobody of a secretary had trapped one of Italy's most gorgeous bachelors? Could she really cope with that level of insecurity, on top of dealing with sharing an apartment with the irascible tycoon?

'Okay, I'll wear your ring,' she said, as if she didn't really care one way or another.

CHAPTER TEN

'I've made an appointment for you to see the doctor today,' Vito announced one morning, by way of a greeting. 'Can you be ready for ten?'

'*Today?*' Flora looked up from the *cornetto marmellato* she was tucking into, wiping her greasy fingers on the pristine linen napkin. Since she'd arrived in Milan, her nausea had completely deserted her and once again she was doing justice to her favourite meal of the day—though a rather elevated version of what she was used to. Fresh fruit, delicious juices and pastries which were baked right here in Vito's apartment and which appeared like magic whenever she sat down for breakfast. It felt like a long way from Ealing.

This morning, she had been eating alone in the splendour of Vito's high-ceilinged dining room, until the tycoon's unexpected arrival had shattered her solitude—and her equilibrium. She placed the napkin down on the table, surprised—yet again—by the flash of fire against her flesh. The enormous diamond engagement ring—which had arrived by courier yesterday morning—sparkled like a burst of rainbow. But it was as heavy as a rock and she was still trying to get used to the weight as it kept spinning around her finger.

'Why not today?' he drawled, in answer to her question.

'I saw a doctor just before I left England,' she objected. '*And* I had a scan. I don't need another one.'

'You're in Italy now,' he asserted firmly. 'And I want you to see an Italian doctor. The best in the city, I'm assured. He can see you at eleven and one of my assistants will accompany you.'

Frustratedly, Flora put the remains of her cornetto down. Her appetite had suddenly fled and not simply because Vito had marched in here being his usual bossy self. The sight of him would tempt a saint and she wasn't feeling particularly saintlike at the moment, because—along with her more conventional appetite—had come a burst of sexual hunger which was now making itself very evident in the urgent prickle of her breasts. How annoying that he still had that effect on her. Or that her pregnancy hadn't dampened down her desire for him.

Clad in his trademark suit, his thick hair still damp from the shower, it was hard for Flora not to ogle him. He had (presumably) been up at his usual ungodly hour, because Mafalda had explained what his morning routine involved. A vigorous session in his gym was followed by a half an hour's swim in the rectangular pool set in the verdant roof terrace. An actual swimming pool which overlooked the actual Duomo because that was the kind of preposterously over-the-top detail which creative architects provided for their impossibly wealthy clients, apparently. After that, he would disappear—

either to his study on the ground floor—but more often to his company headquarters near the Via Vincenzo Monti. Signor Monticello was, Mafalda had informed her, a *stacanovista*—which was the same as the English word *workaholic*.

It was, Flora acknowledged glumly—one of the few Italian words she could pronounce perfectly. Perhaps she needed to learn the ones for *indifferent*, or *distant*—which could also be applied to Vito Monticello with equal accuracy, because hadn't he been going out of his way to avoid being alone with her for any length of time? Why else would he have gone on 'urgent' business to Bologna and Roma and Capri, not arriving back home until long after Flora had crawled into her comfortable bed.

She had been here for four days and done nothing but eat and sleep, but deep down she'd known that she'd needed the rest. It had been recuperative to wake up late and have Mafalda fuss around her like a mother hen, as she provided the most delicious breakfast. Afterwards she would find a book in Vito's vast library and take it onto one of the terraces to enjoy in the spring sunshine. She was working up to venturing out on her own, but all in good time. And at least she no longer resembled the haunted-looking woman who had arrived here. She just hadn't realised how exhausted she had been.

'One of your *assistants*?' she echoed incredulously, dragging her attention away from the sensual curve of his lips and focusing on his preposterous suggestion instead. 'Is planning on coming to the doctor with me?'

'Her name is Chiara.'

'Are you having a laugh?' Flora glared at him. 'I'm not going to see the doctor with one of your assistants!'

'She's about your age,' he said reasonably. 'And she's great fun. I think you'll like her.'

But Flora wasn't in the mood to be reasoned with, nor to willingly accept Vito's glowing praise of another woman. 'Whether or not I like her is irrelevant. She's not the right person to be accompanying me.' She drew in a deep breath and suddenly she knew she wasn't just going to sit back and accept his blatant evasion. 'It should be you.'

Six feet and two inches of muscle-packed masculinity stilled as a pair of icy-blue eyes regarded her incredulously. 'Me?'

'Why do you say it as though none of this has anything to do with you?' she demanded exasperatedly. 'You're the daddy, aren't you? You were the only man present at conception.'

'That's not funny, Flora,' he warned dangerously.

'Oh, I know you've been doing your best to keep me out of sight and mind, like some brood mare,' she continued, as if he hadn't spoken. 'But don't you want to be involved in some way, Vito?'

'No.'

But despite the forbidding tone of his response, Flora refused to be deterred. 'They're bound to give me a scan. Aren't you interested—even if it's from a purely intellectual point of view—to see what your son or daughter looks like on a sonar screen?'

'Not particularly,' he snapped, but only after a telltale moment of hesitation.

'I don't believe you,' she said softly. 'And I think you'd be crazy to miss out on this opportunity, even if you never want to repeat it.'

She could see a muscle working at his temple before he finally threw his hands up in the air in exasperation. 'Oh, very well. Have it your own way. I'll come, if you insist!' he growled, as he headed for the door. 'Especially if it means I won't have to endure this kind of tirade before I've even had a cup of coffee. Be ready for ten,' he said icily, calling for Mafalda to bring him some coffee to his office.

After slamming his way out of the dining room, Vito stormed upstairs to his office, which enjoyed commanding views of the Italian city. But for once his morning was exceedingly unproductive. Scarcely bothering to engage with any of the emails which had flooded into his inbox overnight and refusing all but the most vital phone calls, all he could think about was Flora and her feisty determination to involve him in her pregnancy.

And didn't every fibre of his being object to that? Wasn't that why he had been going out of his way to keep his distance from her? Not just because he couldn't look at her without wanting her, but because he was afraid. He, who was never afraid—now found himself terrified of being sucked into the mess of a relationship which had the potential to detonate the hard-fought-for calm of his life.

He was mainly silent as the car took them to the San Raffaele Hospital in the north of the city and they were ushered into the gleaming quiet of the obstetrics department. But when he glanced down and saw Flora biting her lip, he found himself wondering if she were anxious. And something in the apprehension which clouded her face made his heart miss an inexplicable beat. Had he arrogantly concluded that she would be taking all this in her stride—and was it that which made him suddenly reach out to squeeze her hand, feeling totally undeserving of the look of gratitude she shot him in response?

But his brief gesture of comfort seemed to have given her unspoken permission to grab his hand again as her belly was covered with jelly and the sonographer began to track a small instrument over her stomach.

Vito tried to study the screen with scientific detachment—to assess the contrast between light and shade, because that was a lot easier to get his head around, than believing that this pulsing form was a real-life embryo. Flora was looking at him expectantly as if she wanted him to speak but for once in his life he couldn't think of a thing to say. Or maybe that was because, incomprehensibly, his throat had thickened and he didn't want her to know that.

Afterwards, they were summoned into the offices of Professor Aldini, where Flora underwent a brief examination. 'Would you like to know the sex?' the medic queried, directing the question mainly at Vito.

This time the look Flora shot him was easy to discern. Clearly irritated by the sense of masculine collusion in the room, she gave a barely imperceptible shake of the head.

'*Non, grazie,*' answered Vito smoothly.

'We're big fans of surprises,' said Flora, straight-faced, but she gave his hand another squeeze.

They walked out into the waiting room to the sound of someone exclaiming his name and Vito glanced across the plush waiting room to see Arianna Bertini sitting on one of the sofas, staring at him in amazement and his heart sank as he spotted the wife of one of his oldest friends. He could see the incredulity on her face—as well as something which resembled relief and delight. As if seeing him in this particular situation was something which was long overdue. Once again he imagined the weighty chains of domesticity wrapping themselves around his ankles and failed to suppress a shudder.

'*Cosa fa qui*, Vito?' she asked him, starting to rise to her feet rather cumbersomely, given that she was heavily pregnant.

'Please, don't get up,' instructed Vito in English as he reluctantly introduced the two women. 'Arianna, this is Flora—my fiancée. Flora—Arianna is married to Raffaele, who I've known pretty much forever.'

'You are such a dark horse!' chided Arianna switching immediately to the same language and smiling widely at Flora. 'That is a beautiful ring,' she observed, gazing down at the glittering diamond. 'How pregnant are you, Flora, and when's the wedding?'

'A little over three months,' said Flora, finding her voice at last. 'And we…we haven't decided on any dates yet.'

'Well, I hope we're going to see more of you.' Arianna flashed Flora a warm smile. 'Perhaps you can encourage Vito to bring you to our party next week! It would be remarkable if your famously isolationist fiancé attended for once.' She pulled a complicit face. 'He always *claims* to be working.'

'I'll do my best,' said Flora lamely.

After the calm of the obstetrician's office, the world outside seemed extra noisy and Flora was glad the car was waiting for them kerb-side. She settled back into the seat, suddenly aware that her hands were unsteady, but maybe that wasn't surprising. There had been the slightly disconcerting experience of bumping into one of Vito's friends, but the appointment itself had been a highly emotional experience.

Emotional for *her*, anyway. She'd done it solo back in England, but with Vito beside her it had taken on a whole new significance as she'd watched the baby's heartbeat and seen the movement of the tiny shape. She'd sneaked a glance at the man beside her and for one brief second he had looked as if he were all choked up, and her heart had lifted with hope and joy. But just as quickly, his expression had hardened and the moment to ask him about it had been lost, because they had bumped into one of his friends.

Immaculate Arianna, dressed in pale and perfect silk, with hair which looked as if it might have been professionally blow-dried that very morning. She had stared at Flora as if she had just landed from the moon, though had seemed genuinely welcoming once she had processed the shocking news that Vito was engaged and soon to be a father.

'Arianna seemed very nice,' she ventured as their car gathered speed, sensing that neutral topics were probably wisest, in the circumstances.

'She is.' But the pause which followed seemed weighted and the tightening of his lips indicated undeniable displeasure. 'But now the whole damned city will know and my phone line will be hot with journalists peddling intrusive questions.'

'I thought we'd decided that was inevitable,' she shot back, before softening her stance a little. 'You could try putting a more positive spin on it, Vito.'

His head turned to survey her thoughtfully, as if her heated response had activated a neglected part of his brain. 'Do you want to go to their party?' His eyes narrowed. 'Is that what this is all about?'

It was about a lot more than that, Flora thought, but now wasn't the time to start listing all her other complaints and to question why he seemed to have been going out of his way to avoid her. He might tell her truthfully that he found her dull company and she would be forced to live with that knowledge!

'Yes, I would, as it happens,' she said, unable to suppress her sudden leap of pleasure at the thought of an evening out with him. But just as quickly came a wash of social anxiety as she remembered what Arianna Bertini had been wearing and found herself comparing it to Amy's brightly coloured cast-offs, all of which were getting a bit too tight. Would it sound as if she were on the take if she brought such a mundane matter to his attention? Surely it was more a case of not wanting to let him down than being materially ambitious. 'But I'm not sure that any of my clothes will be suitable,' she ventured cautiously.

'Oh, *that*.' Leaning back against the plush leather seat

of the limousine, he gave a quick nod, as if this were a subject he approved of—the ability to solve problems with the use of his wallet. 'That can easily be remedied. We'll just have to buy you some new ones.'

'By next week, you mean?' she questioned uncertainly.

His smile was unashamedly arrogant. '*Si*, of course. By tomorrow, should you wish it.'

'So, what's this party in aid of?' Flora questioned in a low voice, as an attendant took her coat and she and Vito headed towards the party.

'Why are you whispering?'

'I wonder,' she said sardonically, as her eyes darted to an instantly recognisable social media star who was clinging to the arm of a high-profile British politician. 'You don't think it might have anything to do with the fact that everyone here is so famous?'

'I agree it's a fairly glittering segment of society, but so what?' Vito murmured, aware that his voice sounded unusually indulgent but weirdly enough, that was the way he was feeling towards her right now. Protective, yes—that had kicked in from the moment he had discovered that she was pregnant—but also very turned on, in a way which seemed magnified beyond his understanding. His throat dried as he averted his gaze from the ripe curve of Flora's bottom. *Santo cielo!* He wanted to follow her round the room like a puppy dog and not let her out of his sight. He wanted to peel that pale green dress from her petite form. And suddenly he was angry with himself.

Why bring her to a damned party when all he really wanted was to take her to some dark corner, alone and unobserved, where he could give into his wildest fantasies. Fantasies which had been building all week, no matter how much he tried to suppress or deny them. Or maybe denial was what had fed them to a point where he had become a victim of his own frustrated desire. Because she looked...

His throat thickened.

She looked amazing.

Her sleeveless dress was made of pale green silk the colour of a pistachio, which clung like melted butter to her delicious body. The scooped neck provided a distracting glimpse of creamy cleavage and was so cleverly cut that only the most discerning eye would have noticed the faint expansion of her waist. But to Vito—she might as well have carried a sign screaming out the fact that she was pregnant. Her hair was as shiny as glass, her skin full of bloom and vitality and her green-gold eyes were sparking more brightly than the huge diamond ring on her finger. In a sea of svelte women clad mainly in monotone shades of grey and cream, Flora stood out like a handful of rubies spilt on snow.

'It's a birthday party for Raffaele,' he said at last, as he struggled to remember what her question had been.

Her lips framed a shape of mild alarm. 'Oh, no! We haven't even bought him a present!'

He shrugged. 'He doesn't need anything.'

'Ah. I see. Another man who has everything, I suppose?' she validated mockingly. 'Just like you?'

But right then Vito didn't feel like a man who had

everything, despite the apartments and houses, the factories and planes, and the small island off the coast of America which he had rewilded after making his first billion. The one thing he really wanted was tantalisingly within his reach and yet totally beyond it.

Her bright eyes were darting around the room and a small smile was curving her rosy lips. He had sensed her excitement growing over the past few days, as she had gained more of a foothold in his life. And he had allowed her to do just that, hadn't he? Or maybe he had been less diligent about keeping her at a distance after the extraordinary experience of seeing his baby on the ultrasound. Hadn't that driven home the fact that this was all real, and no amount of burying his head in the sand would change that?

But that fact didn't change *him*.

He was still the same man. Still unable to give her what she would ultimately need. But for now, at least, that certainty was weakened by his unwilling fascination for her. Was she aware of how much he wanted her and that every fibre of his being hungered for her, with a taunting lust which rippled through his body? That night after endless night he fantasised about her as he'd thought of her, alone in that great big bed? Yet it had provided some small crumb of comfort that he had not sought her out. A reassuring reminder of the steely control which had always defined him.

'There are so many people here,' Flora observed, plucking a canapé from a passing tray and popping it into her mouth. 'How do you know Raffaele?'

'We were at school together.'

'What, here? In Milan?'

'No. In Rome.' He paused, because she was looking at him expectantly. 'I went to live there with my mother and brother, when my parents divorced. It's where the Italian film industry is based.'

She nodded. 'And what was it like growing up, as the child of an actor?'

She had slid the question so effortlessly into the conversation and if it had been anyone other than Flora, he might have quashed it with an arrogant suggestion that perhaps she was moonlighting as a journalist. But something about the noise of the party seemed to absorb the words as he spoke them, soaking them up like blotting paper, so that it felt less like a confidence and more like the relaying of a simple fact.

'It wasn't easy,' he answered. 'My mother's ambition never really matched her aptitude for acting and for that I think she suffered. We all did,' he added on an aside, his voice hardening. 'Particularly my brother.'

'Oh?'

'He was only a baby when they split,' he informed her, a shiver of distaste rippling down his spine as he recalled the chaos of his parents' messy divorce. 'And my mother wasn't really there for him.'

'Do you mean mentally, or physically?' she ventured.

Vito glowered, angry with her for asking and angry with himself for letting himself talk about it. He had said too much. Why had he said *anything*? She was still looking at him curiously when a woman dressed like a prison guard approached them with a tray and Vito huffed out a sigh of relief at being able to sidestep further questioning. 'What would you like to drink?'

'Just something soft, please.'

And the crazy thing was that her smile was so sweet as he handed her a glass of lemonsoda that Vito couldn't stay angry with her for long, although he was watchful when Arianna came across the room to give Flora a brief hug.

'Flora, you look wonderful,' she exclaimed. 'And those shoes!' Lifting her gaze from the green suede, their hostess slanted Vito an enquiring look. 'Raffaele and some of the others are in his den, watching the end of the Serie A match. I know, I know—but it *is* his birthday! You could join them if you like, while I borrow your fiancée and I could introduce her to some people? There are at least three other pregnant women in the room and we could all discuss obstetricians!'

In a different life and at a different time, Vito might have eagerly agreed to this suggestion, much preferring to watch the football match with his friends and leave the women to their own devices—allowing Flora to flash the diamond he'd given her and bask in the admiration of her peers. And if it had been any other woman, she might have done that. But Flora just wouldn't do that, he realised, even if their engagement *had* been of the more conventional type. Instinct told him she didn't see him as a trophy, or as the route to an affluent lifestyle. She didn't seem to care about that kind of stuff, and suddenly Vito didn't want to offload her as if she were an accessory, or an unwanted burden.

He didn't want to let her go.

'I think I'll keep my fiancée company,' he said easily, placing his hand in the small of her back, and her smile was glittering as she turned her face up to his. 'Shall we go and circulate and behave like the perfect party guests, *cara*?'

'Why not?'

Flora could feel the hard pounding of her heart as Vito took her around the room and started to introduce her to the great and the good, recognising that something had changed. It wasn't a big deal, but it felt like a significant one.

He was touching her.

It was the lightest and most innocuous touch imaginable, but it was the only thing she was conscious of. As if he had set her cold skin on fire with the molten flame of desire which was never far from the surface. Yet hadn't he always had that effect on her? In the Laird's lodge her reaction to him had been instant and overwhelming—she'd never experienced anything like that in her life. And now she had tasted the pleasure he was capable of giving her—didn't that make her desire for him even more intense?

In a daze, she tried to stay in the moment as Vito introduced her to people. She met the social media star who had been clinging onto the politician, and several members of a football team everyone seemed to assume she would have heard of, but hadn't—which caused a moment of hilarity among the assembled guests.

Everyone was charming and Flora was surprised to find herself quickly feeling at ease. Maybe that was more to do with the man beside her and the way everyone seemed to regard him, though she noticed the brief bemusement on the faces of the other guests when he introduced her, as if Vito had confounded all their expectations by getting engaged to this unknown Englishwoman. That he was her *fiancé*.

She found herself saying the word out loud—rolling it around her mouth as though it were a fine wine. Because wasn't she allowed to pretend for once that this was a normal relationship? With Vito's light touch never leaving her waist, nor him her side—wasn't it acceptable to play the part expected of her?

It was almost midnight by the time they got back to the Piazza San Babila and the apartment was completely quiet, save for the ticking of a distant clock. They stood in the entrance hall, where one of the staff must have left two small lamps on, so that the vast space was soft with apricot light and dusky shadows.

'Thanks for a lovely evening,' Flora said formally, her fingers digging into the green suede clutch bag which matched her shoes exactly.

'You enjoyed it, I think,' he observed, with equal formality.

'Mmm. I haven't stayed up this late for ages.' She yawned, perhaps a little self-consciously, trying to inject a little normality into an unreal situation as she met the gleam of his eyes. Something about the fairy tale quality of the subdued lighting and the memory of his touch was making her unwilling to move. But she wasn't going to be needy, or open herself up to unnecessary hurt by letting him know that. He was the one who had set all these silent rules in place, wasn't he? A light touch to the small of her back was hardly an indication that he was now filled with a raw and unstoppable passion! 'Goodnight, Vito.'

His gaze bored into hers. 'I wish it didn't have to end,' he said suddenly.

'Do you?' she taunted softly. But she didn't move, just continued to stare at him. She was aware that this had become a silent battle of wills—or should that be willpower?—and she knew the precise moment of his capitulation. She could sense it in the almost imperceptible change in his big body. The way his muscles tensed and he sucked in an unsteady breath.

But still Flora waited. Even though she was desperate to touch him, she needed *him* to make the first move. Because something told her that was important. That this wasn't just about sex, it was about power. And so far Vito had nearly all the power in their relationship—if you could call it a relationship. Couldn't she taste some of it for once—by silently inviting him to do something she knew he wanted just as much as she did?

She tilted her chin upwards and heard the silken whisper of her hair as it brushed against her shoulders and suddenly the man who was all about cool composure cracked, like a sheet of thin ice beneath the hard stamp of a foot. With a low growl he moved forward to take her in his arms, pulling her close to the beat of his thudding heart as he bent his head to crush his lips to hers.

CHAPTER ELEVEN

'FLORA...' VITO'S VOICE was unsteady as he halted his urgent examination of Flora's silk-covered breasts—closing his eyes as another spear of lust arrowed through him, temporarily rendering him incapable of coherent speech.

Somehow they'd made it to his bedroom after some very hot and hungry kissing in the hallway, which had made him feel about seventeen again. He'd heard Flora urging him on with slurred and broken entreaties as her thighs had parted, which had made him realise that if he wasn't going to push her up against the wall and take her right there and then, then they needed to change the location. Because, even though they were alone in the house he didn't want this to be fast and furious, with her panties on the floor and his trousers around his ankles. He wanted to take it slow. To revel in the delectable body which had been sending his blood-pressure soaring for days now.

Yet for the first time in his life, he felt at a disadvantage as he stared down into her upturned face. 'None of the usual rules apply, do they?' he husked unsteadily. 'You're pregnant and...'

'And what?' she interrupted, her voice as shaky as his. 'Pregnancy isn't an illness, Vito. I'm healthy and fit and young. The doctor I saw in England told me that it's perfectly okay to have sex.'

'You were told *that*?' he questioned, a little outraged.

'Of course. Don't be such a prude.'

'I have never been accused of that before,' he objected.

'There's a first time for everything.' She giggled as she stood on tiptoe and he could feel the warmth of her breath on his jaw. 'I just want you to treat me normally, Vito,' she whispered. 'Please, don't make allowances.'

But what was normal? Vito wondered dazedly—counselling himself against tearing off her dress, and instead sliding the zip down so that she stepped from within the concertinaed circle of green fabric and stood before him in her lingerie.

For a moment he just drank her in.

The soft curves and luscious flesh, fractionally more abundant than last time he'd seen her like this.

He removed her shoes and stockings and carried her over to bed and he thought he heard her purr with satisfaction, as if she were enjoying this macho display of masculine domination as much as he was. She lay there watching him—her legs indolently splayed and her arms pillowing her head to showcase her pert breasts to their best advantage, as if she had just been reading a manual on how best to turn a man on without touching him.

'I want you,' he growled, as he kicked a shoe across the bedroom and tore off a silk sock.

'I sort of gathered that,' came her demure reply.

With another uneven laugh he removed his own clothes—though never had such a task seemed so onerous as he tugged them from his body with careless disregard. At last he sank down beside her and unclipped her lacy bra—tossing it aside along with the matching panties. And when she was naked he pushed the ruffled hair away from her cheeks so he could give his full attention to the rosy lips which were pouting in his direction.

He kissed her for as long as it took for her to grow restless, then played with her swollen breasts until she was shivering with need, but still he took it slowly, even though the effort of holding back was nearly killing him. He drifted his hand over her belly—still very flat, he observed—until he had located the honey of her waiting folds and she almost leapt off the bed as he began to tease his fingertip over her tight little bud.

'Vito,' she whispered.

'I like it when you say my name like that,' he confided with satisfaction.

'L-like what?'

'Like I am your master.'

'Th...that's outrageous,' she gasped, reaching down to encircle him within her fist, as if eager to demonstrate that she was perfectly capable of making *him* weak with longing.

And she was.

Santo cielo—was she trying to get him to come before he was even inside her?

'I want you now,' he declared hungrily, moving over her to ease himself inside her wetness and groaned as he felt her tight muscles contract around him. With a single stroke, he filled her completely and now she was moaning too as he began to move. 'I'm not wearing a condom,' he bit out.

'I'd noticed,' she whispered conspiratorially, her thighs tightening around his back. 'We don't need to, do we?'

'No,' he growled. 'We don't.'

It was the first time in his life he hadn't used protection and Vito wondered if it was that which made what was happening feel so unbelievably mind-blowing. It must be. What else could it be? But very soon he was past thinking, concentrating only on silencing his own carnal needs to focus on Flora's pleasure before indulging his own. But he was on a knife-edge of desire as he thrust deep inside her and never had it been so difficult not to come.

Even when she began to convulse around him, he held back—though whether that was to reinforce the mastery of his own body, or to enjoy the spectacle of watching her orgasm, he wasn't sure. But he *did* watch her. Saw the way her lips opened in delight and her cheeks and breasts bloomed like roses. Her arms tightened around his back and he could do nothing but give in to his own hunger at last, shuddering helplessly as his body jerked out his seed.

Afterwards he rolled off her and pulled her close, his arm locking comfortably around her waist as he felt the first velvety beckon of slumber. He must have slept—he didn't know for how long—only that when he opened his eyes the moon had moved across the sky and Flora was lying there, bathed in moonlight, a small smile of satisfaction curving her lips.

'Did you enjoy that?' he questioned, bending his mouth to one silver-tipped nipple which instantly puckered beneath his questing tongue.

'Mmm.' She wriggled a little, parting her thighs as if to encourage the hand which was resting on her belly to move downwards but her voice was a mixture of shy and curious. 'What took you so long?'

'You want me to be faster next time?' Deliberately misunderstanding, he began to finger the honeyed folds, but if he thought pleasure might divert her line of questioning, he was wrong.

'That's not what I meant.'

He sighed, giving himself up to the inevitable. 'I kept away from you because I figured that platonic was best for both of us, for all the very obvious reasons.'

'And they are?'

'Oh, come, Flora.' He slid a finger over one slick fold, suspecting she knew his reasons very well. 'You really want me to spell them out?' he taunted.

'Y-yes,' she gasped.

'Sex is a complicating factor in an already complicated relationship.'

'I agree. So what happened?' she whispered. 'What changed your mind?'

'Are you just angling to hear me say that I was wrong?'

'Only if it's true.'

There was a short pause. 'Yes, it's true. I can't seem to resist you,' he gritted out reluctantly. 'Satisfied?'

'Um...'

Vito was laughing as he bent his head to her breast once more but a momentary ripple of unease whispered over his skin, because he wasn't used to humour in the bedroom. Was it that which made him take it even slower than before, reassuring himself that his steely self-control remained intact—until Flora was writhing and whispering words into his ear which were turning him on even more?

'Please, Vito,' she gasped.

'What is it that you want?' he teased softly, and he could see she was very close to the edge...

'You know what I want,' she breathed. 'You.'

'Well, since you asked so nicely...' With another hard thrust she began to spasm around his aching shaft and he was ambushed by his own release. He found himself choking out incomprehensible words as he lost himself deep inside her and afterwards, he lay there, too dazed to think, or even to speak—because that had been sex on a whole new level. He pushed a damp strand of hair away from her forehead.

'Mmm,' she murmured as she opened her eyes. 'That was nice.'

'*Nice?* Is that a classic example of English understatement?' he demanded.

'Okay. That was a poor choice of adjective. It was amazing. You know it was.' She gave a big yawn. 'But I guess I ought to think about getting back to my own room.'

His territorial instincts aroused, for women rarely took the initiative about absenting themselves from his bed, Vito edged his finger around the kiss-swollen outline of her lips. 'Why?'

She gave the fingertip an absent lick before moving her head away. 'Because if I don't I'm going fall asleep and stay here all night and that might cause problems in the morning.'

'What kind of problems?'

With difficulty, Flora held back an impatient sigh, wondering if he was being deliberately dense. She wasn't going to lie to him. Besides, it would have been difficult to fabricate anything when she felt as if he had stripped her bare in more ways than simply the physical. Beneath his gaze and touch, she had felt completely exposed and that had been scary and wonderful, all at the same time. It had been the most incredible sex of her life—even better than last time, though maybe that was because Vito had been more tender than she remembered. Or was she guilty of seeing things she wanted to see, rather than things which were really there?

'Because then your staff will get even more confused,' she said. 'They are used to us having separate bedrooms.'

'So what? I don't live my life pandering to the sensibilities of my staff.'

What about mine, she wanted to object, *but that would definitely smack of neediness.*

'They'll think we're a couple—a real couple,' she persisted. 'And we're not, are we?'

There was a pause and his eyes narrowed, as if she were laying down a trap he had encountered many times before. 'You know the answer to that, Flora,' he answered silkily. 'But I see no reason why we can't enjoy each other's company while you're here.'

'You mean like friends—with benefits?'

He gave a slow smile of delight. 'That's exactly what I mean.'

Flora absorbed the subtext to his heartless statement. They could have all the sex they wanted and then, when she left, he would presumably bid her a civilised farewell and move on with the rest of his life. That was always what he had intended should happen, she reminded herself savagely—he wasn't backtracking on anything he'd already said—her stay here was never intended to be anything other than a temporary refuge. But although there was no point in castigating him for his rigid stance, Flora suddenly found herself wanting to understand it.

'So, what happened to make you so opposed to relationships?' she questioned curiously. 'I mean, I know your parents had an awful divorce but that happens to lots of people, and they don't all end up living like monks. And before you start looking at me like that, I'm not trying to get you to change your mind! I'm just trying to understand you better so that when our child asks about you—as he or she inevitably will—I'll be able to talk about you naturally, instead of just coming up with a blank.'

He grimaced at this projection of the future and Flora thought he might try to shut the subject down by kissing her, or telling her that he needed to sleep. But maybe he recognised the validity of her argument, because his heavy sigh was accompanied by a brief nod of resignation, although Flora didn't miss the bitterness which flashed in his eyes.

'Last night you asked me what it was like living with an actor and perhaps I was also guilty of understatement,' he began. 'If you must know, it was hell. After the divorce, my mother's acting work dried up. The offers just stopped coming in. I don't know if my father had anything to do with that—he was a powerful man and he found it hard to forgive her.'

Forgive her for what? Flora wondered but she didn't ask, she just let him continue with his story in that strange, flat voice she'd never heard him use before.

'As her looks faded, so did her ability to attract men. So, in the absence of any consistent confidante, she used to confide in me.' His mouth twisted with something which looked like contempt. 'One night, after too much brandy—she informed me that my little brother was the product of an affair, but that nobody knew. Apparently, Alessandro's father was the owner of one of the film studios, who refused to leave his wife for her. She said my father had always suspected she had been unfaithful, but couldn't prove anything. It was in the days before DNA tests were popularised and anyway, they divorced when my brother was still a baby.'

'But why did she tell *you* all this?' questioned Flora.

He shrugged. 'Maybe she wanted to offload her conscience. Or maybe she knew that I'd witnessed them screaming at each other and was just confirming the accusations I'd overheard.' He shuddered. 'She said I must keep it secret and so I did. That's when I learnt the skill of compartmentalising. I locked that knowledge in a place in my head and never told anyone—until my mother was long gone and my father was on his deathbed and begged me to substantiate what he had always suspected. And so I did.' There was a long pause as he looked at her bleakly. 'Because how can you possibly lie to a man who is dying?'

'I'm guessing the answer is that you can't. You're damned if you do and damned if you don't,' she whispered.

'I thought that carrying her guilty secret had been the only burden I had to bear,' he continued and now there was a hollowness to his words. 'Until my father cut my brother out of his will. Despite the fact that I'd made my own fortune, he left everything to me. And my brother, who hadn't had an easy passage in life— got nothing. So Alessandro came to me, demanding to know why he had been shunned, asking me whether I knew the reason. And I found that I couldn't lie to him either. Because what right did I have to play god and deny him the knowledge of his true father, even though he had died many years before?' His voice cracked a little, like the splinter of long-neglected wood beneath the heavy blow of an axe.

'I explained that I didn't want or need our father's money and to prove it, I transferred every last Euro of his fortune into Alessandro's account, but that didn't seem to make any difference. He was angry with our mother, and with my father and of course, angry with me—because everyone likes to shoot the messenger, don't they? And he turned all that rage in on himself. He started to use drink and drugs to blot out the pain and there was nothing I could do to stop him. I loved my brother,' he added brokenly. 'But within a few short weeks of Papa's death, he was almost unrecognisable.'

'Oh, Vito,' said Flora, but he barely seemed to notice the fingers she gently touched to his cheek in an instinctive gesture of compassion. It was as though he had pulled the cork from a bottle of long-suppressed emotions and now they were spilling out in a dark and bitter stream.

'One night he phoned me up to rage that life wasn't worth living and the very next day he drove his car into a tree and died instantly.' He swallowed. 'And I don't think it was an accident.'

'You're not blaming yourself for what happened are you, Vito?' she asked him as she registered the almost unbearable pain in his voice. 'Because you must know we are only ever responsible for our own actions and not for anyone else's.'

'You think it's that easy?' he demanded roughly. 'Yes, I do feel responsible. Of course I do. My family was a total mess and I should have kept well away from the fallout of my parents' toxic relationship. I can't help but wonder what would have happened if I'd lied to Alessandro and told him I knew nothing about his parentage. Whether he would still be alive.'

'Don't you think everyone does that? That at some point in our lives we find ourselves wishing time had a rewind button?' Flora demanded. 'I remember I had a bad cold when Mum went off on her last climb and I used to think that if I'd asked her to stay, then she wouldn't have been caught in that terrible storm on the mountain. But you can't turn the clock back and even if we could, it still might have turned out completely differently.'

'Yes, I know all this,' he said impatiently. 'But you need to know why I treat coupledom like kryptonite, Flora. Because families are just a path to pain and loss. People get hurt and I don't want to be around that kind of emotion, ever again. Do you understand?'

Yes, she understood but Flora saw little point in trying to dispute his cold-blooded certainty by pointing out that there were always exceptions. She'd asked him the reasons behind his aversion, not to try to talk him out of it. And since he had told her, he must trust her to some degree—and wasn't that an unexpected bonus? So, instead of talking she wriggled closer, placing her hand on the flank of his hip and it felt like something of a victory that he didn't push her away. She held her breath as some of the tension left him and when she let her fingers drift over his belly, a different kind of tension entered his body.

When she inched her fingers down to clasp his rocky shaft within the palm of her hand, he groaned. And soon after that she climbed on top of him and took him deep inside her, orchestrating their movements with the clench of her muscles, until at last he cried out and pulled her down so he could claim her lips in a hard, sweet kiss.

And in the end, the question of whether or not she should stay the night became academic because next time Flora opened her eyes, it was morning and the space beside her was empty.

Pushing the hair back from her face she surveyed the room. Her expensive silk dress was lying on the rug, next to a pair of abandoned suede shoes, and there was Vito's immaculate dinner suit beside them—carelessly discarded. Flora bit her lip with remembered pleasure and leaned back against the pillows as Vito walked in.

He was completely naked—long, muscular limbs emphasising his strength and power. He moved like the natural predator he was, she thought—this golden alpha man who made women's hearts hurry. The richness of his skin gleamed like oiled-silk and his black hair glittered with tiny beads of water, which he was rubbing at with a tiny white towel. But despite his undeniable magnificence and the abundance of thrills he had given her throughout the night, it was the fact that he had confided in her which gave her an inner glow. Hugging that knowledge to herself like a precious gift, she smiled up at him.

The smile he slanted back was lazy and contented—like a leopard at the zoo which had just been fed. As he raised his ebony brows at her in mocking question, Flora could feel the flush of colour in her cheeks as he walked over to the bed and dropped the towel. Keep it light, she told herself. Don't scare him away with feelings.

'So, *cara*, what do you say?' he murmured. 'Friends with benefits, *si*?'

He got into bed beside her, his mouth tracing a slow line down her neck and Flora would have defied any woman on the planet not to have agreed to his drawled suggestion.

CHAPTER TWELVE

'You aren't wearing your engagement ring.'

Meeting Vito's curious stare from across the other side of the table, Flora quickly glanced down at her bare finger. To be honest, she'd completely forgotten she wasn't wearing it but probably explained why her left hand felt so delightfully liberated this morning. 'Oh, I took it off yesterday when I was helping Mafalda make focaccia—'

'You were helping Mafalda make bread?' he elucidated, his surprise apparent.

'Yes. She's a brilliant cook and she's offered to teach me. She practises her English and I practise my Italian—and all the time I'm getting insights into Italian cuisine and life. And it means I've got something to do while you're working all the hours god sent,' she remarked, without rancour.

'*Vero*,' he agreed, picking up his newspaper and using it as a clear deterrent not to progress with this particular topic.

Faced with the black-and-white barrier of financial news, Flora pushed her plate away, knowing she hadn't been completely transparent with him. She could have explained that not only was the ring too heavy for her finger, or that the stone would have become encrusted with dough—she also felt it was a bit *vulgar*—when all Mafalda wore was a narrow wedding band which somehow seemed a lot more meaningful than the expensive gem *she* sported. Or that she'd been in a store the other day and seen someone covetously eyeing up the glittering rock, and had been terrified they might try and cut her finger off and make away with their prize. And yes, one of Vito's bodyguards had been standing at a discreet distance away, but even so—it had rattled her. Why hadn't she told Vito the truth—that she had never really liked it?

She knew why and the reason was making her feel increasingly uncomfortable. Because the easy honesty she'd once enjoyed with her ex-boss had slipped away, like sand trickling through an egg-timer, and Flora knew the precise moment when it had happened.

When they'd started having sex again.

Because sex was about so much more than release.

It was about power, and bargaining and control. Those were the downsides...

The upsides were the incredible vulnerability and intimacy which flooded through her whenever she was lying next to Vito, skin on skin. When she felt as close to him as she could possibly be and revelled in the blossoming confidence of her own sexuality. When she started wondering if this strange relationship of theirs could go the distance. Or if it could ever turn into love.

She bit her lip, alarmed by her residual foolishness

and resolving to push it to the edges of her mind. Because what was the point of going *there*?

The room was flooded with pale sunshine which turned Vito's thick hair blue-black, and the air was richly scented with coffee. On the table were bowls of fruit, creamy yoghurt and freshly baked *cornetti* and Flora was aware that the scene could have been lifted straight out of a romcom film about a newly married couple who were expecting their first child together.

Except that they weren't married and they weren't a couple.

Friends with benefits, yes—and she wasn't *complaining* about that aspect of their relationship. Why would she? She got to sleep with Vito every night and wake up next to him. And sometimes, during those private hours of darkness she was exposed to aspects of his character which would never have revealed themselves in daylight. Occasionally his hand would skate across the faint curve of her belly and Flora would hold her breath, waiting for words about the baby which never came. The elephant wasn't in the room so much as in her stomach, she thought wryly. Only then, he would start making love to her again and she would be able to think of nothing but his touch.

Yet sometimes he made space for her in his busy diary and they did things together, and those were the days she treasured above all else. He showed off his adopted city and the surrounding areas and she grew to adore Italy. They ate in amazing restaurants or drove out to Lake Como or Bergamo, and Vito seemed to enjoy her bemusement when they explored the more avant-garde collections in Milan's many art galleries. All this was intoxicating stuff—but in the most unexpected of ways.

When a man like Vito was helping you on with your coat and enquiring solicitously if you felt okay, it could be just as mind-blowing as when he had his head between your thighs and was exploring you with the evident enjoyment of someone flicking their tongue over an ice cream cone. Just like sprawling on sofas reading, or watching something on TV, or having the Italian tycoon massage the soles of her feet before bedtime could make Flora's heart want to burst with joy. It could feel worryingly like a *real* relationship and it wasn't. He had warned her against that from the get-go.

And he had demonstrated that in other ways too, hadn't he?—deliberately erecting barriers intended to keep her at an emotional arm's length. Those confidences he had shared about his family were a thing of the past and every follow-up question she'd dared ask had been shut down with a cool and icy precision. He was adept at wearing a mask of indifference, just as he'd been doing since he'd first come downstairs this morning. Did she sigh? Was that what prompted his next question?

'Is everything okay, Flora?'

She shrugged. 'I suppose so.'

Vito lowered his newspaper as he suddenly became aware that her gaze was burning a hole in it. As her green-gold eyes regarded him unblinkingly, he felt his throat grow dry—a familiar frisson of surprise rippling over his skin. Because even though she'd been living in his apartment for almost a month and they ate breakfast together most mornings, it still came as something of a shock to see her sitting there in the cold light of day.

'Sure?' he persisted. 'You seem a little preoccupied this morning.'

'No. Everything is fine,' she said.

He nodded, running his gaze over her, satisfied that scooping her up and rescuing her from that crummy little flat in Ealing had been for the best—because wasn't the evidence sitting there and glowing before his eyes? Pregnancy had made her bloom, he thought, with a beat of satisfaction. Her hair had never looked more lustrous, nor her skin so fresh and clear. At first he'd wondered if the knowledge that she was pregnant with his child would destroy his sexual hunger for her, but to his surprise, his desire for her remained as powerful as before. And didn't the darkness provide a welcome respite from the thorny questions about what was going to happen in the future? Throughout their passion-filled nights, it was easy to forget how much remained unsaid.

His mouth hardened.

So much unfinished business.

The date for her departure and his role—if any—in the life of their child were still to be decided, and he sensed they were both reluctant to raise a subject which could destroy this fragile compatibility they had created.

Sooner or later they were going to have to confront it.

But not today.

'So how are you planning to spend the morning?' he questioned idly.

She dabbed at her lips with her napkin. 'Amy's calling me in a while for a chat.'

'How is she?'

'She's fine. Loves Brisbane. Likes her new job. Brett's teaching her how to surf. All good stuff.' She folded the napkin and put it on the table. 'Then later, there's a baby shower for Luisa and Arianna is giving me a lift there.'

'*Eccellente.* Enjoy,' he said indulgently, rising from his chair and walking round to her side of the table to bend his head to kiss her.

Flora watched him go and something about the perfunctory kiss he deposited on top of her head made her feel slightly indignant. As if she were some sort of appendage, rather than a person! 'I'll do my best,' she said, a little pointedly but naturally, he didn't hang around to continue the conversation—he was already out of the door on the way to the office. His beloved office!

She slipped on a light cashmere jacket which matched her new linen dress—because her wardrobe had expanded, although her baby bump was still barely noticeable. She was now almost sixteen weeks pregnant and Professor Aldini had pronounced himself delighted with her progress. Even Amy had seemed mollified during their last phone call, comforted by the fact that her big sister was living in unbelievable luxury in one of the most gorgeous cities in the world, and that Vito was ensuring she was well-cared-for.

But she hadn't told Amy what she was only just beginning to admit to herself.

That she wasn't sure how much longer she could carry on like this. Hiding away her true emotions behind an air of pragmatic calm. The guilt and the fear which ambushed her at random times and eroded the excitement she felt at the thought of having Vito's baby. Knowing that the birth would be the beginning, but also the end and they couldn't carry on pretending that the future didn't exist.

She knew they ought to address when she was actually going to leave, but it was easier to put off discussing a subject which filled you with horror. Easier to pretend there wasn't a bomb ticking away in the background and that some time she was going to have to think about going back to London. Alone.

Flora did her best to push these mixed-up thoughts from her head, endeavouring to be good company as Arianna drove them to Luisa's home—a charming eighteenth-century house in the Brera region, although the usual stunning view of the botanical gardens was partially obscured by a sea of pink balloons and ribbons.

As Flora walked into the large reception room, she was greeted with genuine affection by some of the women she'd met since she'd been living in the city. Arianna and her friends had shown her nothing but kindness and she liked them very much, although at first she'd been forced to work her way through a minefield of expectation as they asked her questions she couldn't—or wouldn't—answer. They seemed to find it incredible that Vito Monticelli was in a relationship at last but Flora couldn't bear to enlighten them that it had never been a relationship, just a festive one-night stand—with consequences. Terrified of provoking their pity or concern, she couldn't bring herself to disclose the cold-blooded nature of their arrangement.

She settled down to enjoy a sugar-rush from one of

the local *canestrelli* cookies, along with a cup of peppermint tea. There were several women she hadn't met before and one in particular seemed eager to chat. Beatrice Maresca was the girlfriend of someone called Alessio Cardini and Flora screwed up her nose because the name rang a bell.

'I haven't met him, but I've definitely heard of him,' she said.

'Yes, you would have done,' replied Beatrice, in her perfect English accent. 'Vito goes skiing with Marco and Alessio every Christmas.' She pulled a face. 'Only this year they've added some extra dates to the diary. Because their ski trip was cut short—poor darlings!— they've decided to go salmon fishing in Iceland in October! And October just happens to be when I have my birthday. How outrageous is that?'

It was also when a tiny baby would be barely a month old.

Flora's fingers crushed her cookie and a shower of fine crumbs was immediately demolished by Luisa's tiny dog. And now Beatrice was asking was everything okay, because she'd gone so *pale*? And Flora told her that everything was fine, hoping that her brittle smile was reassuring. Somehow she managed to hold it together during the drive home, though her responses to Arianna were little more than monosyllabic and she heaved a sigh of relief when she reached Vito's grand apartment, grateful to be on her own.

Politely telling the staff that she neither wanted nor needed anything, she paced around one of the vast reception rooms, as she waited for him to come home, feeling at a loss. With a heavy heart she acknowledged that she'd been walking on a tightrope for all these weeks and she knew the time had come to talk to him.

To say what?

She hadn't decided.

Pace, pace, pace over the polished wooden floors she went, wondering if some sixth sense had warned Vito that she was on the warpath and he'd deliberately chosen to work even later than usual as a result. She knew how much he loathed 'scenes' because he had taken great pains to inform her, and up until now she hadn't felt inclined to complain about a situation she had voluntarily signed up for. But something had happened today in that balloon-filled room. She'd had some kind of epiphany and her restraint had flown out of the window, so that by the time Vito walked into the reception room where she was lying on the sofa staring sightlessly at a magazine, she couldn't contain her rage.

'Here you are—at last!' She threw the magazine down and his eyes narrowed.

A pair of black eyebrows swooped upwards. 'Is something the matter, Flora?'

His cool, almost indifferent query only added fuel to the fire and Flora sucked in a deep breath, knowing it would serve her purpose better if she stayed calm—but any type of serenity seemed to be beyond her as all her repressed emotions bubbled to the surface. 'You're going fishing in October!' she accused.

Vito almost laughed because she made his pursuit of salmon sound as reprehensible as if he'd acquired another mistress and was keeping two of them concurrently on the go. But he didn't laugh. He might often have been accused of coldness but he wasn't stupid and he could see she was angry—angrier than he'd ever imagined she could be.

'Yes, I am,' he agreed. 'Do you have a problem with that?'

'Do I have a problem with that?' she echoed. 'Vito, what are you thinking? You do realise we'll have a newborn by then?'

A single word leapt from out of her diatribe and hung there in terrible isolation, like the blade of a guillotine, hovering above his head.

We'll.

How could one small word assume such inappropriate and presumptuous significance?

He raised his eyebrows. 'And?'

But his determination to remain cool didn't have the desired effect because she leapt up off the sofa as if it was contaminated.

'*I* don't have the luxury of going away on some luxury trip!' she accused him hotly. 'Because I'll be looking after a baby.' She paused and sucked in an angry breath before staring at him very steadily. 'Your baby.'

In the beat which followed Vito felt a sense of panic rising up inside him and he dealt with it in a way which had always proved fail-safe in the past. 'You will have childcare help around the clock,' he assured her. 'You know that.'

'Oh, for goodness sake! That's not what I'm talking about!' she objected. 'You're still in denial, aren't you?

You haven't actually accepted that this baby is really happening—whether you like it or not!'

He shot the words out like bullets. 'Things will get back to normal.'

'But that's where you're wrong, Vito. They won't. Not like you're used to. Not like before. It's going to be a completely different kind of normal. I know that from when I had to care for Amy. Nothing will ever be the same.' She hesitated. 'And deep down, you probably don't really want it to.'

Her voice had grown almost gentle and in many ways, Vito found that more difficult to deal with than her anger.

'What are you talking about?' he questioned forbiddingly.

'I think you already love this baby more than you know.' She took a step towards him and instinctively, he tensed. 'I saw your face when I was having a scan,' she informed him softly. 'I saw how choked up you were.'

How *dare* she try to second-guess him, he thought furiously. To put herself inside his head and tell him what he was *thinking*, instead of listening to what he was actually saying to her. Wasn't this his worst nightmare come true—all the mess and misunderstanding of human emotion, right here—in his home, like a nest of hornets? Didn't that cancel out the surprising fact that living with her had been more delightful than he'd ever expected?

Because *this* was the reality of letting a woman into your life.

The breath in his throat was raw and ragged and now

he felt the hot burn of guilt. Damn her—why was she making him feel so *guilty*? 'I made the fishing arrangements a while back,' he stated coldly. 'Before you even came to live here. And even then, I was pretty sure you would have returned to England before the birth.'

'You're completely missing the point!' she howled, lifting her hands in the air in obvious frustration. 'You can't just stick us in a box, no matter how much you'd like to. Your baby shouldn't be something you *compartmentalise*!'

Vito felt the quick beat of alarm, knowing he needed to close this down, and quickly. And what better way than with the truth? Even though initially she might find it unpalatable, surely it would be better for her to confront it in the long run.

'Look, this isn't going to work, the two of us,' he said flatly. 'Not long-term. Your stay here was only ever intended to be temporary and nothing has changed. You are a wonderful woman in so many ways, but I cannot be the man or the father you and the baby need, and deserve.'

'What are you talking about?' she whispered.

'I am a cold-blooded and arrogant bastard.' He gave a short laugh. 'Or so I have been told more times than I can remember, and deservedly so. Don't you understand the truth of what I'm saying to you, Flora?'

Somehow Flora met the regretful look in his eyes without flinching, even though her heart felt as if it was shattering into a million pieces. Perhaps he wanted her to flounce out and start packing in a dramatic and pride-salvaging way—that would certainly provide him with an easy let-out clause. But she owed it to their baby to strive for more than that and she owed it to herself too. Because hadn't she grown to love this unconventional and infuriating man—no matter how much she tried not to, nor how hard he tried to push her away?

'Can't we at least give it a go, Vito?' she questioned simply. 'For all our sakes? For what it's worth, I think those signs of cold-bloodedness and arrogance are becoming increasingly rare—'

'And you think that has something to do with you, do you?' he demanded dangerously.

'Why don't you ask yourself the same question?' she enquired patiently. 'I know I have. I think we're good for each other.' She sucked in a deep breath, knowing it was now or never. And yes, this was laying her feelings on the line with a risk of getting hurt—and risk was something she had spent her life avoiding. But some things were worth abandoning your long-held fears for. Wouldn't it be a pyric victory if she walked away now, without telling Vito how she really felt? What price pride or dignity, if she spent the rest of her life feeling miserable because she hadn't dared fight for the man she loved?

'I actually think we might have the basis for a real relationship, and not just the friends-with-benefits thing,' she continued, in a low voice. 'I've seen the layer of goodness you try to hide beneath your grumpy exterior. Most of the time you make me very happy and I don't think I'm mistaken in saying that you seem quite happy too. I also happen to think you'd make a great dad, Vito. I really do. You're strong and funny and clever.' She sucked in an unsteady breath. 'I think we could build a life together—a good life—and if you lifted the blinkers from your eyes, you might realise that too.'

How long did it take for hope to be extinguished?

Only a few seconds, Flora discovered.

As long as it took for that ice-blue gaze to freeze over and for those sensual lips to harden into a cruel and forbidding line. That's when she accepted what an utter fool she'd been.

There was a long pause before he spoke and when he did, it was in a voice Flora hadn't heard for a long time. Not since he'd started at Verdenergia last Christmas and ruthlessly pared back the ailing organisation. When he'd got rid of the festive decorations, along with all the things which weren't working properly—and now he was doing exactly the same to her.

'I'm afraid that's not going to happen,' he said in response to her heartfelt statement, shrugging his broad shoulders and extending the palms of his hands, as if he were offering her the world. 'I can offer you pragmatism, but not permanence.'

'Excuse me?' she said faintly.

'You can have whatever you want, Flora. A house in London. A holiday home too, if you like. As many staff as you think it will take to make your life run smoothly. And a maternity nurse—I gather that's a thing? You will have a generous allowance and I will put a trust into place for the child,' he continued, when she didn't reply.

He was regarding her coolly as if waiting for a response and the only thing Flora wanted to say was—it's *our* child, not *the* child! But that would be spiteful and emotionally manipulative—and hadn't he already experienced enough of that to last him a lifetime?

She bit her lip with frustration and pain. She didn't doubt that she and the baby would thrive without him because she would make sure of that. She'd always been strong because she'd had no choice and she would continue to be strong. Yet maybe she owed it to Vito Monticello to call him out for his behaviour, otherwise he might just get to thinking it was acceptable? 'You think you can just outsource everything, don't you, Vito?' she demanded, in a low, shaking voice. 'That if you throw enough money at something, it will all go away. But deep down, you're a coward.'

'A coward?' he bit out furiously. 'How dare you say this to me?'

'I dare because it's true! Think about it!' she flared back. 'You can just buy your way out of this situation and make the baby go away. You can file us neatly away in a box called *unwanted family*, but I can't do that. I don't want to, but even if I did—I don't have a choice!' She gave a bitter laugh, because somehow that was managing to keep the tears at bay. 'But at least this way I'm free to nurture and love this innocent little scrap without you. I won't need to worry about being openly demonstrative, or commit the heinous crime of actually showing I *care* about you. Maybe I really *should* thank you, Vito,' she added steadily. 'Maybe you've done me and our baby a big favour.'

CHAPTER THIRTEEN

'So...' FLORA CAREFULLY manoeuvred the camera-phone and did a panoramic shot. 'This is the garden. Quite a big plot for a London garden.'

'No way! It looks more like Kew Gardens!' Amy's voice boomed down the line, sounding as if she were in the same room rather than ten thousand miles away. 'Flo—it's absolutely gorgeous! And you've even got *staff.*'

'Well, only a housekeeper,' said Flora, using words which wouldn't have been part of her vocabulary a few short months ago. 'I'm very lucky.'

'Well, I wouldn't go *that* far,' said Amy gloomily.

'*Very* lucky,' emphasised Flora firmly. Because she was not going to hear a single bad word said against Vito. He was still the father of her child and he hadn't actually done anything wrong. He just hadn't been the man she had wanted him to be. If any blame was to be apportioned—then maybe she should accept her fair share, for having had unrealistic expectations. He had never wanted to be a father, but he had done the best he could in the circumstances. 'Anyway, I've got to go,' she said, with a glance at her watch. 'I want to go for a walk while it's still light, but before that I've got some *canestrelli* in the oven which needs rescuing.'

'Come again?'

'They're those Italian biscuits which I've learnt how to make.'

'I'm not even going to ask why you're cooking Italian food.'

'Because I'm taking them to the Babies and Bumps group later.'

'That's not what I meant,' said Amy darkly.

'I know it wasn't. But whatever has happened between me and Vito, I'm not going to deny this baby his or her Italian heritage,' agreed Flora airily. 'Call you tomorrow?'

'Sure.'

Flora terminated the call, took the biscuits out of the oven, told Susan the housekeeper she was going out, and closed the front door behind her as she set off towards the park.

She had been back in England for a whole month, having flown in on Vito's jet before being installed in a penthouse suite at the Granchester Hotel, while a house was found for her. It was weird what money could buy. Apparently there were people whose job it was to find the 'perfect' property for wealthy people and rush through a quick sale, before said property was completely redecorated to exacting specifications.

Which was how Flora found herself living in Richmond—an area of London she'd always adored. There was a park with deer, independent shops and—most important of all, the local nurseries and schools were good and there was a definite sense of community. It would all be fine. She kept telling herself that. And sooner or later she would start believing it.

Vito had telephoned during her first days here and initially, Flora's heart had leapt with a stupid hope she hadn't quite managed to kill off. But the calls had been stilted, obviously motivated by a heavy sense of duty—and she had requested he didn't do so again, unless it was urgent. He hadn't asked her reasons and she was grateful for this one small mercy, not wanting to confess that she found it unbearably poignant to hear his richly accented voice and feel the subsequent regret and longing which washed over her. She'd wondered how she could possibly get over him, if she was constantly being reminded of him?

And somehow she didn't seem able to maintain the distance she supposedly wanted. Why else had she sent him an unasked-for picture of her latest scan last week? Was she hoping for some sort of reaction when he discovered it was a little boy?

The scent of lilac in the park was rich and heavy in the warm May weather and Flora watched as a toddler stumbled in pursuit of a tiny white dog. Should she get a dog, once the baby was old enough? Would that make the house seem like more of a home? She was so engrossed in comparisons between Labradors and terriers, that at first she only vaguely registered someone was saying her name and it wasn't until she listened properly, that she stopped dead in her tracks.

Because only one person said her name like that.

Her heart was pounding as she turned around and

there he was. Dark, and tall and utterly delicious. Right there in Richmond Park, many miles from his Milanese home.

'Hello, Flora.'

She blinked and, for a moment, all she could do was drink in the sight of all that glorious breathing flesh, before her thoughts started flagging up a warning.

What was he doing here? She swallowed. Had he moved on with a new woman and was doing the honourable thing of telling her about it before she found out from someone else?

'Vito!' she said, her voice sounding miraculously calm. 'How on earth did you know where to find me?'

'Your housekeeper told me.'

'Is that why you insisted I hire one, so you'd have an in-house spy?'

'I could have employed plenty of discreet trained bodyguards if I'd wanted to spy on you,' he offered dryly. 'A housekeeper is supposed to make life easier for you, that's all.'

Why on earth were they talking about the housekeeper?

'What are you doing here?' she continued coolly—because cool made it sound like she was in control, even though inside she was anything but. 'And why didn't you tell me you were coming?'

Why indeed? Vito wondered, as he met her quizzical gaze. Had he been afraid she would make herself impossible to find if he gave her any warning? He wouldn't blame her. His heart pounded, his mouth growing as dry as parchment because the sight of her was like a feast to his eyes. Her red-brown hair was piled on top of her head and she wore a dress as blue as the gentian flowers which grew in the Alps, and hinted at the curve of her belly beneath.

She hadn't moved, standing there as confidently as a bouncer in a nightclub, her expression now slightly irritated. 'Well?'

'I got...' He shrugged his shoulders with unaccustomed self-consciousness. 'I got the scan photo you sent me.'

'Oh, right.' For the first time she looked a little flustered. 'Maybe I shouldn't have—'

'Yes,' he interrupted urgently. 'You should.'

'Oh.'

She was still looking at him expectantly and he realised she wasn't going to help him out. Or explain why she'd been living in England for the best part of a month without making a single request that he come and visit her.

Because hadn't he hoped for that—even if deep down, he knew he didn't deserve it? That she would crack first and tell him how much she missed him, and could he please come to her, as quickly as possible. And he would have instantly complied—relieved to be able to do so without the need for self-examination.

But Flora had not begged, or pleaded, or even made a careless request. She had cut him from her life with a ruthlessness which had taken him by surprise, until that photo of his unborn child had arrived last week and his heart had felt as if it were being ripped from his chest and he had asked himself if he was just going to sit back and let this *happen*.

'I have been a fool, Flora,' he said.

'Please don't keep pausing and waiting for me to insert some suitable response, or question,' she said tightly. 'I'm not in the mood to play guessing games.'

Vito nearly smiled at her waspishness, because such a retort was so outside his experience of women that it whetted his appetite for her even more. But then he drew himself up short. Wasn't he arrogantly making the supposition that all he had to do was utter a few cursory words of apology and everything would go back to what it had been like before?

He didn't want it to go back to what it had been like before.

'I told you about my early years and the secrets I was expected to keep,' he began slowly, but her eyes had narrowed in surprise, as if this were not the opening she had been expecting. 'About learning how to compartmentalise my feelings and my emotions. Believe me, if you do that often enough, you can shut them away entirely and I became very good at it. But there were plenty of other lessons which my childhood taught me. I learnt that men and women play games with each other, and that love is a lie. Those were my core beliefs, Flora—and it was very hard to shift them. Indeed, I saw no reason ever to do so.' If she noticed his change of tense, she did not comment on it. 'And then came that night with you in Scotland. The best night of my life,' he added quietly. 'At least, until you came out to Milan—'

'Don't you dare start coming out with a load of old

blarney just because you're sexually frustrated!' she bit out and he was relieved to see some of her brittleness waver.

'Do you really think it's that simple?' he demanded. 'If this was just about sex, don't you think I could have flicked through my address book and found a myriad of possibilities to help me ease it?'

'How dare you say such things to me?'

'Why, does it make you jealous, Flora?'

She stilled and tilted her chin. 'I told you... I'm not going to obey your verbal prompts.'

'I spent a pretty miserable skiing holiday that Christmas,' he admitted bleakly. 'Marco and Alessio kept asking me what was wrong and the last thing I wanted to admit—to them, or to myself—was that I couldn't stop thinking about you. When I found out you were pregnant I was...'

'What?' she questioned, seeming to forget her vow not to prompt him.

Vito's jaw tightened. This part was more difficult. He wasn't going to lie in order to make her feel better, because he suspected she would see right through it. And if he was to have any kind of chance with her, she needed to trust that he would only ever tell her the truth—no matter how painful that might be.

'Scared,' he said, in as frank an admission as he'd ever made. 'My own experience of family life had been hell on earth and I was terrified of recreating that toxic environment. I convinced myself that you and the baby would be better off without me, but what I hadn't factored in was the inexplicable truth...' He stared into her extraordinary eyes. 'Which was that somewhere along the way—without my permission, or even my comprehension...' He gave a hollow laugh. 'I had fallen in love with you.'

He thought that any other woman—suddenly secure in the knowledge of how much he cared for her—would have thrown themselves into his arms, rather than increasing his uncertainty with their continued silence. He thought about what best to do. What did they call it? Grovelling. Yes, that was it. Some of his friends had told him they'd been forced to do it before a woman would consent to marry them, but he'd never imagined himself joining their number. He searched her expression for some reprieve but seeing none, was forced to press on.

'When I came to find you in Ealing, I thought the reason I was so insistent you return to Milan with me was to ensure you and my unborn child were safe and that I was doing the right thing for you both. Which was true. But there was an undeniable element of victory there too. I was triumphant to have got my own way, because I like to win.' He gave a bitter laugh. 'Yet ironically, it wasn't until you had left Milan that I realised I was no winner. In fact, I was losing the only thing that mattered. Which was you. Is you. Only you and always you, Flora.' He swallowed, the words making his throat constrict. 'If you would have me.'

Still she said nothing and now their eyes were on a collision course, her green-gold gaze burning into him, like fire.

'Will you have me, Flora?' he questioned brokenly.

'Could you love me too, after everything that I have done, or failed to do?'

Maybe Flora should have made him wait some more. Should have taken a moment to revel in this new and shining realisation of her own feminine power and the fact that he loved her. But the urgency of her answer was as vital to her own well-being as drawing in the next breath of air. She didn't underestimate what it had taken for a man like Vito Monticello to reveal these things to her. For a buttoned-up man who mistrusted emotion, it was about as big a deal as you could get.

'I've loved you for a long time, Vito,' she answered quietly. 'To be honest, I don't think it's in my power to stop loving you.'

'Then you must marry me,' he commanded, a low growl of exultation rumbling from him, as he pulled her into his arms.

'Oh, yes,' she whispered. 'Hell, yes.'

And despite the fact that they were in broad daylight, standing in the middle of the park, Vito's mouth was on hers and he was kissing her like a man who'd never kissed before. In fact, people had stopped to stare at them, prompting Vito to lace his fingers with hers to take her back home, where she discovered he'd given Susan the rest of the day off.

'Do you really think it's your place to mess with my staff?' she teased him.

'Why? Is there something else you'd like me to mess with?' he murmured.

They were both breathless by the time they reached the bedroom, to a vast bed which had only ever been occupied by one person. Vito's fingers were almost reverential as he peeled off the gentian dress and the look in his eyes as he drank in her fecund nakedness made Flora's heart turn over with love and longing. And then it was her turn to undress him, her fingers fumbling with her eagerness to have him close again.

And there, in a room filled with rich sunshine which warmed their skin and turned it to gold, Vito pulled her into his arms, and Flora knew this was the beginning of the rest of their lives.

EPILOGUE

THE BEACH WAS SILVER, long and very beautiful.

It was also very private, which was one of the reasons they'd chosen it.

Neither Flora nor even the much-travelled Vito had ever been to Australia before, thus making it the perfect place for a honeymoon, albeit a very delayed one. Because although babymoons had their place—a holiday was much more fun when you weren't pregnant.

Mind you, thought Flora as she let out a sigh of satisfaction, and surveyed the sleeping profile of her husband, she sometimes thought she could have been incarcerated in a coal shed with Vito Monticello and she would have been happy.

Everything he did made her happy.

As she did him. Or so he told her.

They had married very quietly in London, before Tommaso's birth. Vito had been eager to make her his wife as quickly as possible and neither of them had wanted any fuss. No cheesy celebrity magazine articles about Italy's most eligible man being snapped up by his unknown English bride! The diamond ring had been sold, with the proceeds going to charity, and Vito had replaced the disliked solitaire with a delicate concoction of emerald and yellow sapphires, which Flora adored. The Richmond house had gone straight back on the market and Flora had sold her Ealing apartment to Joe, at a very favourable price and he and his boyfriend were currently knocking it through, to turn the two flats back into one house.

Baby Tommaso had been born in Milan—a long and sometimes difficult birth—but Vito had been there for her at every step of the way. Flora would never forget the way he had gripped her hand and mopped her brow, his face grimacing with helplessness as she'd shuddered through another contraction. Or the unashamed brightness of pride and joy in his eyes as he cradled his newborn son and whispered *grazie* into her mouth, as he bent his head to kiss her. And she had been right when she'd thought he would be a good father. He was a *brilliant* father—kind and patient and entertaining.

Now their boy was a sturdy and adorable toddler who was currently staying with his doting auntie Amy and uncle Brett while his *madre e padre* enjoyed their first proper break as a married couple. Flora missed their son like crazy but she knew it was good for her and her husband to have time on their own, just as it was good for Tommaso to explore the world without them always by his side. She'd wondered at first whether Vito's candid examination of his feelings when he'd asked her to marry him would be a one-off. Whether he would revert to his old ways of emotional restraint once he had got his wish of making her his wife, but that hadn't been the case. It had been the beginning of something very beautiful. A closeness with her ex-boss which went beyond her wildest dreams.

With him, she could talk about anything and everything and, despite her rapid acquisition of the language and her growing circle of friends in Italy, Vito was still the person she most wanted to spend time with. The person she most enjoyed eating dinner with. Her lover. Her soulmate. Her best friend. He'd even cancelled his fishing trip and told her that such male-only pursuits were to be postponed, until he could take his young son with him.

And, in the most dramatic turnaround of all—she'd even got him to enjoy Christmas—and to *admit* that he had enjoyed it! With their baby son just three months old, they'd held a huge party in their Milanese apartment and Flora had worn the pale pistachio dress her husband was especially fond of, while outside the bells of the Duomo had exuberantly rung in the New Year. She loved Milan but lately they'd been spending more and more time in Vito's beautiful Tuscan castle and she suspected they might move there full-time if and when their little family expanded, which both of them were hoping would happen very soon.

Long, ebony lashes fluttered open and Flora basked in the smoky blue gaze she knew so well. Vito's magnificent body was completely naked and she feasted her eyes on the silken olive flesh...the broad shoulders, rocky torso and long, powerful thighs which had inspired so many delicious fantasies...and realities.

'You know what happens when you stare at me like that, don't you?' he teased lazily.

'Do I?' she enquired innocently, tracing the outline of his mouth with her finger. 'You were asleep for ages.'

'I know.' He pushed a strand of sea-damp hair from her face. 'But I'm wide awake now.'

'Mmm.' Her cheeks grew pink. "I can tell.'

Vito expelled a low groan of pleasure as he brought her up against his hungry body. Flora. Sweet, beautiful Flora. She had transformed his life with her passion and the glorious gift of their beautiful son. She had taught him things he'd never known—and only when he'd learnt them did he recognise their importance. How to relax and live in the moment. How to appreciate the simple things in life. He'd even drastically cut back on work to spend more time with his family. He loved her so much that his heart sometimes felt as if it wanted to burst right out of his chest. Every second in her company was pure gold.

He told Flora he loved her every day of his life, but, as he nudged his thigh between hers, Vito knew there was something vastly more satisfying than telling.

He smiled.

He liked to *show* her...

* * * * *

If you were captivated by
Christmas with Consequences,
*then be sure to check out these
other dramatic stories from Sharon Kendrick!*

Italian Nights to Claim the Virgin
The Housekeeper's One-Night Baby
The King's Hidden Heir
His Enemy's Italian Surrender
Greek's Bartered Bride

Available now!

Get up to 4 Free Books!

We'll send you 2 free books from each series you try PLUS a free Mystery Gift.

FREE Value Over $25

Both the **Harlequin Presents** and **Harlequin Medical Romance** series feature exciting stories of passion and drama.

YES! Please send me 2 FREE novels from Harlequin Presents or Harlequin Medical Romance and my FREE gift (gift is worth about $10 retail). After receiving them, if I don't wish to receive any more books, I can return the shipping statement marked "cancel." If I don't cancel, I will receive 6 brand-new larger-print novels every month and be billed just $7.19 each in the U.S., or $7.99 each in Canada, or 4 brand-new Harlequin Medical Romance Larger-Print books every month and be billed just $7.19 each in the U.S. or $7.99 each in Canada, a savings of 20% off the cover price. It's quite a bargain! Shipping and handling is just 50¢ per book in the U.S. and $1.25 per book in Canada.* I understand that accepting the 2 free books and gift places me under no obligation to buy anything. I can always return a shipment and cancel at any time. The free books and gift are mine to keep no matter what I decide.

Choose one:
- ☐ **Harlequin Presents Larger-Print** (176/376 BPA G36Y)
- ☐ **Harlequin Medical Romance** (171/371 BPA G36Y)
- ☐ **Or Try Both!** (176/376 & 171/371 BPA G36Z)

Name (please print)

Address   Apt. #

City   State/Province   Zip/Postal Code

Email: Please check this box ☐ if you would like to receive newsletters and promotional emails from Harlequin Enterprises ULC and its affiliates. You can unsubscribe anytime.

Mail to the Harlequin Reader Service:
IN U.S.A.: P.O. Box 1341, Buffalo, NY 14240-8531
IN CANADA: P.O. Box 603, Fort Erie, Ontario L2A 5X3

Want to explore our other series or interested in ebooks? Visit www.ReaderService.com or call 1-800-873-8635.

---

*Terms and prices subject to change without notice. Prices do not include sales taxes, which will be charged (if applicable) based on your state or country of residence. Canadian residents will be charged applicable taxes. Offer not valid in Quebec. This offer is limited to one order per household. Books received may not be as shown. Not valid for current subscribers to the Harlequin Presents or Harlequin Medical Romance series. All orders subject to approval. Credit or debit balances in a customer's account(s) may be offset by any other outstanding balance owed by or to the customer. Please allow 4 to 6 weeks for delivery. Offer available while quantities last.

Your Privacy—Your information is being collected by Harlequin Enterprises ULC, operating as Harlequin Reader Service. For a complete summary of the information we collect, how we use this information and to whom it is disclosed, please visit our privacy notice located at https://corporate.harlequin.com/privacy-notice. Notice to California Residents – Under California law, you have specific rights to control and access your data. For more information on these rights and how to exercise them, visit https://corporate.harlequin.com/california-privacy. For additional information for residents of other U.S. states that provide their residents with certain rights with respect to personal data, visit https://corporate.harlequin.com/other-state-residents-privacy-rights/.

HPHM25